DECATUR HOUSE

and Its Inhabitants

The End Papers are prints taken from original drawings by Benjamin Latrobe. The first drawings are for the Entrance Hall and those at the end of the book are for the Drawing Room.

DECATUR HOUSE

and Its Inhabitants

by

MARIE BEALE

1954

TABLE OF CONTENTS

FOREWORD

At a reception given at Decatur House on May 1, 1953, for the Trustees of the National Trust for Historic Preservation, Mrs. Truxtun Beale announced her intention to bequeath to the Trust the house, with many of its contents, together with an endowment for its preservation as a national monument. By this far-sighted and generous act, Mrs. Beale has assured the future of this important building which is noted not only for its historical associations but also as a fine example of American architecture of the early Federal period.

Decatur House was designed by Benjamin H. Latrobe, architect of the United States Capitol and also of Saint John's Church on Lafayette Square. During the latter part of the Nineteenth Century, Decatur House suffered certain minor alterations. In 1944, Mrs. Beale retained the services of the well-known architect, the late Thomas Waterman, and arranged for the facade of the house to be restored to its original condition in accordance with the drawings of Latrobe which had come into her possession.

Now Mrs. Beale has added still further to the value of her gift by writing, out of her own knowledge and from sources available to her, this interesting account of Decatur House and its occupants. She gives a vivid picture of social and political events that have taken place in the house, beginning with Stephen Decatur's opening ball in the great double drawing-room, and continuing through the occupancy of many notable personages, including a Russian Minister, three Secretaries of State, a Vice President, a British and a French Minister, and lastly during the ownership of General Edward Beale and his son, the late Truxtun Beale and his wife, the present owner of Decatur House who has added lustre to the long and brilliant tradition of the mansion as a center of social and political life in Washington.

It is important that the facts, as set forth in this volume, should be available to the Trust and to the public who will eventually have access to this historic house. We are grateful to Mrs. Beale for having given us this book in addition to her other great benefactions.

DAVID E. FINLEY
Chairman, Board of Trustees
National Trust for Historic Preservation

Washington
August 1954

1818 Decatur House 1944

DECATUR HOUSE AFTER RESTORATION TO THE ORIGINAL LATROBE DESIGNS
AS INTERPRETED BY THOMAS WATERMAN IN 1944.
FROM A WATER COLOR BY C. NYQUIST

CHAPTER I

AMERICAN HERO

DECATUR HOUSE was aglow with light as the carriages of the arriving guests clattered up the gravelled road, recently cut through from Pennsylvania Avenue. A great ball at Decatur House was an event in the social life of early Washington, still a straggling town slowly emerging from the local countryside. Pennsylvania Avenue, the main thoroughfare, was a rough road linking the Capitol and the President's House, and along it here and there were Congress boarding-houses, "with veritable swamps between," as an early traveler wrote. In the entire city there were only a few new residences for permanent inhabitants, and one of these, now just a little more than a year old, was the home of the naval hero, Stephen Decatur. Here on the evening of March 18, 1820, Commodore and Mrs. Decatur were entertaining in honor of the President's daughter.

Commodore Decatur had left his mark on the development of Washington when, with prize money from his naval career, he had built a home a few hundred yards from the President's House. President Jefferson had decided to reduce the size of the Presidential grounds and Decatur purchased some of the land thus made available for private use. It was then an open field or commons, bare of trees, where the local militia drilled upon occasion. It had been owned previously by the Pierce family, part of a tract called Jamaica; nothing was left of the farmhouse of Edward Pierce but stones of the old family graveyard. To the westward was a race-course where the local gentry matched their blooded horses. The neighborhood still abounded in small game; a sportsman recently had written that there was excellent shooting in the center of Washington.

After the War of 1812 the area just in front of the President's House began to acquire a distinctively new character. A landmark here was St. John's Episcopal Church, directly opposite the President's House, and the place of worship for fashionable Washington society. The rector was "somewhat of an original" to his contemporaries; he still wore smallclothes and buckles, and as a militia captain during the war, in command of a company composed mainly of theological students, he had scouted military discipline by refusing to march to Niagara, because he preferred to defend New York. After the war the incident was remembered, and Commodore Decatur refused to attend his services. Shortly after the construction of the church, Decatur's house was built nearby in the year 1818, and he and his wife occupied it the following January. The three buildings, the President's House, St. John's and Decatur's home, served to mark out a square in the rustic countryside. In L'Enfant's plan for the city this area was called President's Square. Not until some years later would it be known as La Fayette Square.

A great deal of careful planning went into the construction of Decatur House. The Commodore retained the services of the foremost architect available, Benjamin Latrobe, an Englishman by birth, who had carved out a career in America. Privateers had ransacked the ship carrying his private library across the ocean, so Latrobe had begun his work in this country with classical designs produced from memory. The building of a city on the Potomac offered a rich field for his genius. He was commissioned to redesign the two main structures in the new capital, the Capitol itself and the President's House. The first buildings on President's Square also were monuments to his architectural dexterity, St. John's and Decatur House, and have a special place, accordingly, in the architectural history of the country.

Conformity with the distinctive location seems to have dictated the design of Decatur House. The President's House was planned by the architect, Hoban, after a style developed in the previous century for the Tidewater countryside, where homes beside the Chesapeake estuaries fronted both ways, toward the water and the land. In sharp contrast, Decatur House was designed as a town house, situated foursquare on a city street, with a façade of elegant simplicity. It was a consciously urban structure that might have graced a London square.

There also was a personal quality in the design, reflecting the life and tastes of a great sea captain. The severely urban residence of Georgian brick was compact and sturdy as a ship, while the re-

2

PORTRAIT OF STEPHEN DECATUR BY GILBERT STUART
*(By permission of the National Gallery of Art,
Smithsonian Institution, Washington, D. C.)*

PORTRAIT OF SUSAN DECATUR, WIFE OF STEPHEN DECATUR,
BY GILBERT STUART
(By permission of Mrs. William F. Machold of Philadelphia)

striction of external ornament to a minimum was consistent with the forthright character of a man of action. This ruggedness endowed the house with a solid dignity, enhanced by the beautiful proportions of the façade. The keynote of austerity was relieved by the quiet graciousness of the entrance, a doorway adequate to welcome presidents, ministers, and naval commanders returned from the sea.

The severity in the façade, however, was suppressed in the design of the interior, which reflected another aspect of Decatur's life. The classic hall led through two archways to a curving staircase with a continuous-rail banister. The central feature of the house consisted of great drawing rooms on the second floor, whose elaborate proportions testified that the builder had in mind the function of the house as a center of Washington society. In the rear were the kitchens, slaves' quarters, and carriage houses. The building of such a home in the straggling, swamp-ridden city of the period, when the members of Congress lived in boarding-houses, is evidence of Decatur's vision of a new era in the life of Washington.

On this evening in March, 1820, the Decaturs were giving a ball for President Monroe's daughter, Maria. Nine days before she had married her cousin, Samuel L. Gouverneur, in the first wedding held in the home of the Presidents. After a week's bridal tour, there was a gay schedule of festivities arranged for the young couple, beginning at Decatur House. The arriving guests were received in the large salon that formed an L across the front and side of the second floor. The guests included most of those prominent in Washington society of the time. Among them were many envoys of foreign governments, in diplomatic regalia, and officers of the Navy and Army in regimentals. The Monroe Administration, with whom the Commodore was a prime favorite, was well represented, in addition to personages of unofficial Washington. The ladies, in Empire gowns and heirloom jewels, shone to great advantage in the benign candlelight. The men not in uniform wore green or claret frockcoats, with silk stockings and pumps, and ruffled cravats of white cambric. Some of the couples danced to the strains of the newly fashionable waltz, then coming into favor, though some of the elders were inclined to treat it with disdain. Others preferred to sit and discuss the events of the time: two months before George IV had succeeded to the British throne on the death of George III; there had been a revolution in Spain; the Missouri Compromise had just been accepted; all interesting material for small talk.

The host and hostess of the evening, Commodore and Mrs. Decatur, according to contemporary reports were a brilliant and imposing couple. At forty-one, Decatur stood at the summit of his career, "the Bayard of the Seas," whose fame was known the world over. Among other resounding exploits he had burned the captured frigate *Philadelphia* in the pirate harbor of Tripoli. After the War of 1812, at the second inaugural ball of President Madison, he had laid the battle flag of the defeated British ship *Macedonian* at the feet of Dolly Madison. Later, as Navy Commissioner, he had settled in Washington with his wife, Susan. Mrs. Decatur was the daughter of a prominent Norfolk merchant, well educated and beautiful, and one of the reigning belles of her time. Before her marriage she had been courted by Napoleon's brother, Jerome Bonaparte, but declined the honor. Then she married Stephen Decatur, whom she met when he was being widely feted and dined on his triumphal return from the Mediterranean. "A very accomplished woman, with fine manners and great powers of conversation," she proved an effective wife for the redoubtable naval hero.

The gaiety of the ball at Decatur House was tempered, for some, by a realization of impending trouble. Only a few of the guests knew why the Commodore, despite his affability as a host, was solemn and preoccupied. There was a personal crisis before him. Decatur had accepted a challenge to a duel, and the terms had been agreed upon. It would be pistols on the field of honor, at eight paces. Decatur realized the hazard and had no illusions about the possible outcome. Already on the way was an urgent message to his wife's family, saying that the affair might prove fatal, and requesting his wife's father to come to be with her. During the ball he remarked grimly to Commodore Porter, who was scheduled to entertain the Gouverneurs next, "I may spoil your party."

A guest that evening in March has left in his memoirs a little sketch of the occasion. Newly returned from diplomatic service

4

in London, Benjamin Ogle Tayloe was impressed by the memorable scene before him. The company assembled in a semicircle about Mrs. Decatur, who played the harp for them. In the center of the semicircle was the Commodore himself, handsome in his naval uniform. His eyes were fixed devotedly upon his beloved wife, a slim figure in her flowing gown, her fingers moving over the harpstrings. His surroundings at this moment were the climax of a brilliant career, his house, his wife, his friends, his guests. In his mind was the chilling realization that he might never again enjoy a scene like this, listening to music in the candlelight.

All the events of his life, in a sense, were part of a complex chain of circumstances leading up to this moment. Stephen Decatur was born January 5, 1779, on the eastern shore of Maryland, in a small country house situated near the ocean, in what is now the little Maryland town of Berlin, originally Burleigh or Burleigh's Inn. His mother had gone there to escape an epidemic of smallpox in Philadelphia or else to avoid the British army under General Howe that had taken the city in 1777. Born to his profession, Decatur was the son of a sea captain who, in the subsequent naval war with France, seized the first prize ship to be captured by the newly-constituted American navy. The elder Decatur was a comrade-in-arms of such figures as John Paul Jones and Commodore Truxtun, while the younger Decatur represented the second generation of the American navy, which included among others Commodores Hull, Perry, and Bainbridge. Young Stephen grew up in Philadelphia and became a midshipman in 1798. After three years of service, mainly in the West Indies, he sailed for Tripoli as a lieutenant, first on the *Essex* and then on the *New York*. He came unscathed through his first duel, wounding his opponent, the mate of a merchant vessel. On the field of honor another time, he acted as second for Midshipman Joseph Bainbridge, who killed his adversary. For their part in the affair Decatur and Bainbridge were sent home, but a few months later Decatur was back in the Mediterranean again, in his first command, the *Argus*, and then the twelve-gun schooner *Enterprise*. In his first action against the Barbary pirates he seized a small corsair vessel and conceived a daring plan of action against their fortified stronghold, the harbor of Tripoli.

The American fleet in the Mediterranean under Commodore Preble, an energetic and irascible New Englander, had cause for deep concern when the Barbary pirates captured one of their finest frigates, the *Philadelphia*. Under the command of William Bainbridge, it was pursuing an enemy vessel when it ran on an uncharted shoal. Listing and unable to maneuver, the *Philadelphia* soon was surrounded by enemy gunboats, and after strenuous efforts to save his ship Bainbridge finally surrendered, with 22 officers and 315 men. The captives found themselves in a Moorish prison, while the frigate was added to the Dey's navy, at Tripoli. To avenge this disaster, Decatur proposed to Commodore Preble a raiding party into the harbor, and was placed in command of the expedition. He and his crew disguised themselves as Maltese seamen, and sailed for Tripoli in the Moorish vessel he had captured, under orders from Preble to burn the *Philadelphia*.

A northeast breeze ruffled the dark waves of the Mediterranean as the 60-ton ketch of Moorish design boldly approached the African shore. Standing on deck were Decatur and his pilot, along with a handful of sailors. Hidden under hatches was a picked group of about sixty men, well armed and ready for a daring venture. As the little vessel, renamed the *Intrepid,* scouted the harbor reefs of Tripoli the men on deck could see the lights along the shore, as well as the dark outlines of the fortress that dominated the harbor. But what they sought was another shadowy form, the hull and towering masts of an American ship. As they drew closer, they could make out the outlines of the frigate *Philadelphia.* Decatur knew her well; his father had been her first captain. Now she lay there helpless under the guns of the fort, with pirate ships nearby.

The key to the enterprise was trickery and daring. Success depended upon surprise, and Decatur had the movement carefully planned. The *Intrepid* was allowed to drift close to the captured *Philadelphia* under cover of darkness. When they were hailed, the pilot replied in Maltese with a well rehearsed story that the ketch had lost her anchors. He requested permission to tie up alongside, and the unsuspecting watch aboard the *Philadelphia* passed a line to the small ketch. Quickly the resolute boarders swarmed over the bulwarks. Alarmed screams of *Americanos!* came too late;

BURNING OF THE "PHILADELPHIA" BY LIEUTENANT STEPHEN DECATUR
IN THE HARBOR OF TRIPOLI, 1804

Decatur's conflict with the Algerine at Tripoli.
Reuben James interposing his head to save the life of
his commander

the corsairs on the ship were overpowered. Decatur and his men rapidly began to fire the *Philadelphia*. When the flames reached the rigging the boarding party dropped back into the ketch, and started pulling away. The work had taken only twenty minutes. Now the flaming vessel lighted the harbor, and enemy batteries began opening fire. The men on the *Intrepid* labored hard on their straining sweeps, while cannon shot fell around them. Finally they pulled out of range, and escaped without the loss of a man. To the American captives in the dungeon ashore the blazing frigate was "a sublime sight."

Decatur's feat, said Commodore Preble, was "beyond all praise," a verdict confirmed by the great British admiral, Lord Nelson, then blockading the French at Toulon, who called it "the boldest act of the age." Congress rewarded Decatur by voting him a presentation sword, and he was immediately promoted to captain. Many expected that Congress would reward him more substantially with prize money for the destruction of an enemy ship, but this was never done. The anticipated prize money, however, is still regarded in the Decatur family as rightfully his due, and is bequeathed from generation to generation.

A popular painting by Carter illustrates another incident from the Barbary Wars. In a bombardment of Tripoli later the same year, Decatur commanded a division of the fleet under Commodore Preble, and captured an enemy ship in a violent boarding action. Meanwhile his brother, Lieutenant James Decatur, going aboard a corsair vessel that had surrendered, was treacherously killed. Enraged at word of this, Decatur maneuvered his ship alongside the enemy, and there was another hand-to-hand engagement. Struggling with the corsair captain, Decatur fell to the deck, but managed to pistol his opponent. At the same time his life was saved by an American seaman who blocked a scimitar blow from another Tripolitan. This episode, too, became widely known, and added lustre to Decatur's name.

He took part in much fighting against the Barbary pirates, commanding for a time the frigate *Constitution*, affectionately known as "Old Ironsides." When a period of peace ensued, Decatur conducted negotiations with the Dey, and brought the Tunisian envoy to the United States in 1805. By then Decatur was a national hero; widely quoted was his grandiloquent toast which ended, "My country, right or wrong!" As guest of honor at a ball given by her father, he met Miss Susan Wheeler, of Norfolk, and they were married on March 8, 1806. Decatur was appointed head of the Norfolk Navy Yard, and held various commands in domestic waters.

When friction with Great Britain, involving the impressment of American seamen, culminated in the War of 1812, Stephen Decatur put to sea once more. This time, however, the enemy was not the Mediterranean pirates but the greatest naval power in the world. Of the 686 British vessels in active service at the beginning of the war, 75 were in American waters. Against these the American Navy could muster but 16 ships in all. Despite the intrepidity of American commanders in single ship actions, it was impossible to prevail against such odds. They scored some notable successes, nevertheless, before the British gained control of the sea.

Decatur was one of the American commanders who helped to ruffle the complacency of the British Admiralty. He sailed from Boston in the autumn of 1812, in command of the frigate *United States* and the accompanying brig *Argus,* which he dispatched to cruise alone. Off the Canary Islands, on October 25, he encountered the British 49-gun frigate *Macedonian,* a fine ship, freshly overhauled. The British ship opened the action at long range, which was a disadvantage against the 54-gun *United States.* When the range closed, Decatur maneuvered with precision, keeping the enemy under intense diagonal fire. After much carnage the *Macedonian* surrendered, having lost a third of her crew. Decatur repaired the prize and brought her back to an American port.

During these early months of the war the heavily-outnumbered American Navy registered a series of victories. Commodore Hull in the *Constitution* defeated the *Guerriere,* and Commodore Bainbridge in the same frigate won a victory over the *Java.* Commenting on these engagements, the London *Times* remarked drily: "It seems that the Americans have some superior mode of firing." But the next year the British frigate *Shannon* defeated the *Chesapeake,* and the preponderance of numbers was decisive.

The American frigates were bottled up in home ports for the duration of the war.

Decatur, chafing under this enforced inaction, watched for an opportunity to run the British blockade, though he knew it was an almost hopeless enterprise. The months slipped by, and on Christmas Eve, 1814, the war was terminated by a treaty of peace signed at Ghent. But communication was slow and hostilities continued until the news arrived. During this period Decatur made a brave but futile effort to break through the blockading squadron at New York. In command of the *President* he put to sea January 14, 1815, in a northwest gale, hoping for protection by the weather. Unfortunately the *President* immediately grounded on a bar and suffered some damage, proceeding at reduced speed. At dawn the frigate was sighted by the British squadron, which set out in tenacious pursuit. The *President* outran them most of the day, but by evening the leading pursuer, the *Endymion,* was within range. Decatur turned to give battle, and the *Endymion* was crippled in a running engagement. But his own ship did not go unscathed, and when other ships of the British squadron drew close it was evident that the *President* was lost. Decatur, who had been wounded in the battle, struck his flag without further action. Later a naval board credited him with the victory over the *Endymion,* and absolved him for the loss of the *President.* The war was over.

In the Mediterranean, however, there was more work for the American Navy. The pirate states on the northwest shores of Africa had been tolerated for a long time by the various European powers, who secretly encouraged them against other powers. For some time the United States paid tribute to protect its trade with the Levant. After it had freed itself by force from the scourge of Tripoli the same difficulty continued with Algiers. Now it was decided to smash completely the system of Mediterranean piracy. In May, 1815, Decatur sailed for Algiers with a squadron of nine ships. Destroying the Algerian frigate *Mashuda* and killing the Dey's admiral, he presented the American peace terms and concluded a treaty that ended forever the tribute from the United States. The American Navy had broken the power of piracy in the Mediterranean. In Rome the Pope declared that "All

Christendom had not effected in centuries what the American squadron had accomplished in the space of a single year."

For Decatur a few years of serenity ensued, after the perils of the sea. He returned to Washington and took up his new duties as Navy Commissioner. With his prize money invested in Washington real estate he was secure and comfortable; the Decaturs had many friends and led an active social life. Childless themselves, they were devoted to Decatur's nieces, the daughters of his widowed sister. Though he took no part in politics, Decatur knew many of the political leaders of the period. On one occasion he pacified his friend General Jackson, who threatened to cut off the ears of Senator Lacock, of Pennsylvania, for speaking slightingly of the Seminole war. Some time during these years he came to the decision to build a home in Washington, and engaged the architect Latrobe for this purpose. On January 16, 1819, Decatur wrote, "I have just moved into my new house." Among the treasures of the house were trophies of his naval career, such as the famous "Decatur plate" and many ceremonial swords presented to him in recognition of his services by various states and cities.

Decatur's career, however, contained a dangerous element, for in the background there was a broken and embittered man, Commodore James Barron, who bore him a grudge that went back many years. In his earlier days Barron had been an outstanding officer with a fine naval career, that included command of the *Essex* and the *President* in the Mediterranean operations. Then an incident occurred that clouded him as a naval officer. He was dispatched to the Mediterranean in 1807 in command of the frigate *Chesapeake*, but was intercepted en route by the British frigate *Leopard*, whose captain demanded the surrender of three crewmen, allegedly British deserters. When Barron refused to comply the *Leopard* opened fire, and Barron hastily capitulated. The *Leopard* took the seamen and departed. The incident, the first defeat of the country's new navy, provoked a storm of rage in the United States, and a court-martial suspended Barron from the naval service for five years, on the ground that he had failed to clear his ship for action. Decatur was a member of this board of inquiry, and thereby gained Barron's enduring enmity.

Quarrels dim with age sometimes are difficult to disentangle. One evening more than ten years later, at his own dinner table, Decatur expressed himself freely on the subject of Barron. The suspended commodore had spent his naval exile abroad, part of the time as an officer in the French Navy. When the suspension period expired the war of 1812 had begun, but he did not return to the United States to take part in it. Barron came back in 1818 and sought a command, but found all roads blocked for him. This he blamed largely on Decatur, who in turn was critical of him for being absent while his country was at war.

Decatur's remarks at Decatur House were repeated, perhaps with malice, and found their way back to Barron in what seems to have been a distorted form. There then began an exchange of recriminating correspondence. On June 12, 1819, Barron wrote from Hampton that he had heard gossip to the effect that Decatur boasted he could insult him with impunity. Decatur replied, denying the remark but giving no satisfaction in his general tone. A number of letters followed, and Barron wrote that he considered himself challenged, after which Decatur conceded that one story about Barron was "unfounded." In another long epistle Barron discussed the ethics of duelling, which he considered a barbarous practice, though sometimes "an appeal to arms" was necessary. Not until January 24 of the following year, however, did the dispute come to a head. Decatur wrote: "If you intend it as a challenge I accept it, and refer you to my friend, Commodore Bainbridge." There was no turning back.

The arrangements were made on March 8, when Captain Jesse Elliott, who was Barron's second, visited Bainbridge aboard the latter's ship, the *Columbus*, at St. Mary's on the Potomac. That same day, which was Decatur's fourteenth wedding anniversary, Bainbridge sent him a copy of the agreement between the two seconds. It provided for a duel on the 22nd of March. Decatur did not allow this to interfere with his social engagements, for during the interval he gave the scheduled ball for the President's daughter, though he was not indifferent to the grave possibilities of the meeting.

In nearby Maryland at the little town of Bladensburg, where the British had defeated the defenders of Washington in 1814, was a famous field known as the "Valley of Chance," the scene of fifty-two duels. The procedure always was much the same: an appointed hour in the morning, seconds to serve the principals, surgeons with bandages, and a brace of pistols. The distance was marked out, final instructions were given, and upon a signal the principals fired. Thus at Weehawken Aaron Burr killed Alexander Hamilton. At Bladensburg James Barron killed Stephen Decatur.

On the morning of the duel, Decatur arose early and went out to meet Bainbridge and another friend, Samuel Hambleton, at a place near the Capitol. The three breakfasted together and drove out in a carriage along the Bladensburg pike. Soon they arrived at the duelling field. The principals greeted each other civilly and conversed with restraint. Next the few formalities began. The choice of position was determined by lot; Decatur won. Bainbridge then paced off the distance, a mere eight paces. This had been specified by Decatur, so that none could say he had taken advantage of his opponent's weak eyesight; at that distance a blind man scarcely could miss. As the pistols were being loaded more onlookers arrived from Washington. The duellists took their stand. At the command "Present!" the pistols were raised. Bainbridge gave the signal.

The two fired simultaneously, the sound of the guns blending together, and Barron dropped. For a moment Decatur remained standing, as the wisps of smoke wreathed about the barrels; he put his hand to his side and fell. The surgeons and onlookers rushed up to the fallen men. They found Barron wounded in the hip, but not mortally. Decatur was bleeding freely; they realized he was beyond aid.

As they lay on the ground side by side, covered with greatcoats, the two men spoke to each other. "Why did you not return to America," asked Decatur, "when the war broke out?" Barron, who previously had declined to explain "under insult," now answered candidly: he did not have money enough. Decatur protested he would have sent it.

Into the waiting carriage they lifted Decatur tenderly, Bainbridge kissing his cheek. From the window of a Moorish prison he had seen Decatur burn the *Philadelphia*. Another carriage was obtained for Barron, and the sad return from Bladensburg began.

It was half past ten in the morning when they carried Decatur into his house and placed him on a couch in the library to the left of the entrance. Decatur was still in command; to spare his wife and nieces he directed that they be taken upstairs. He refused the doctor's suggestion that the bullet be removed. As the painful hours dragged by, many friends crowded into the room for a last greeting, and he thanked them each. After that he signed his will, and with the spirit of a great commander said he would have preferred death on the quarterdeck. That night he died.

"The verdict of history," declares Paullin, "on the chief points involved in the complicated quarrel between the two officers may be in the end somewhat as follows: that Barron was severely, though probably not unjustly, punished for his offence in the fight between the *Chesapeake* and the *Leopard*; that Barron's reason for not returning to the United States during the War of 1812, namely, that he had not sufficient means to pay his way home is not satisfactory; that the resistance of his fellow-captains to his restoration to duty in 1818-1820 was not justifiable; that in the events that led to his duel with Decatur he was the aggressor; but that Decatur's conduct and correspondence were well fitted to inflame and incite the passion of Barron, for whom he showed a decided hostility."

Many thousands attended the great funeral, virtually the entire population of the Capital, including the President and his Cabinet, members of Congress, mayors of various cities, and foreign ministers and their suites. The procession made its way to the suburb of Kalorama, where the casket was placed in the vault belonging to a family friend. Later it was removed to Saint Peter's Churchyard in Philadelphia, where Decatur's parents were buried.

Decatur House was closed for months. After a period of mourning Mrs. Decatur decided she would live there no longer, and moved away to resume her life in new surroundings. Years later she died in a Georgetown convent. Decatur House, meanwhile, had opened a new chapter in its history.

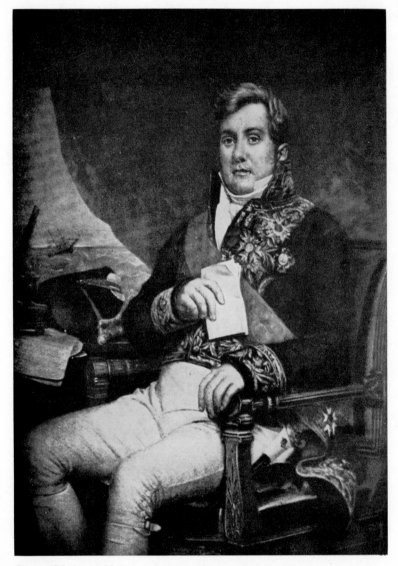

BARON HYDE DE NEUVILLE, FRENCH MINISTER TO THE UNITED STATES

CHAPTER II

ON FOREIGN SOIL

THE FLAG OF FRANCE flew over Decatur House. At the entrance was the plaque of the French Legation. Washington society now entered Decatur House as guests of His Excellency, Baron Hyde de Neuville, French Minister to the United States. It was the year 1822.

Under the usages of international law, confirmed in 1815 at Vienna, Decatur House was no longer under the sovereignty of the United States. The residence of a diplomatic representative was "independent" and "immune," like the Minister himself. It was under French authority and ruled by French law. To all intents and purposes it stood on French soil, as though situated on a Paris boulevard. The whole establishment, from the Minister himself and his Chargé d'Affaires, M. Jules de Menou, down to the French servants and cooks in the kitchen, reflected this transition. The Old World tradition now was housed in President's Square.

At this time the Square was beginning to assume the shape familiar to later generations. It was still an open space or commons until 1826, but surrounding it were several new residences. A house had been built by Richard Cutts, brother-in-law of Dolly Madison, directly across from Decatur House, and there the gracious Mrs. Madison later came to live. When another gravelled roadway was cut through from Pennsylvania, paralleling the one before Decatur House, the Square received its actual outline. In 1824 the aged Marquis de La Fayette paid a triumphal visit to the United States. He was greeted in Washington with elaborate festivities in the Square. From then on President's Square gradually acquired, by popular usage, a new name. Henceforth it would be known as La Fayette Square.

For the diplomatic and social set of Washington the Square was the major focus of their activities, with an endless stream of receptions, dinners and dances. Seven members of the diplomatic set now had the rank of Minister, though for the first twenty years only the French and English Ministers had Washington residences.

"This was the period of the best society in Washington," wrote Benjamin Ogle Tayloe. "Gentlemen of high character and high breeding abounded in both Houses of Congress, and many of the foreign ministers were distinguished for noble birth, talent, learning and elegant manners." He added that "The Baron Hyde de Neuville admirably represented the French aristocracy of the old regime." At Decatur House, after a period of shuttered inactivity following the tragic events of the 1820 season, the French Minister and his wife entertained extensively, and Mme. de Neuville's weekly teas were an institution.

Jean Guillaume, Baron Hyde de Neuville, ardent Royalist and representative of the French nobility, was no newcomer to Washington society, for this was his second diplomatic mission in the United States. He was partly of Scottish ancestry, being descended on his father's side from a branch of the Hyde family that had moved to France. Born in 1776, he grew up as an ardent follower of the Bourbon house, and as a young man, studying in Paris, he was dangerously involved in political intrigue. From 1793 on he was "an active agent of the exiled Bourbon princes." In 1796 he took part in the Royalist uprising in Berri, and four years later, after being acquitted of a charge of conspiracy, found it expedient to spend a period of voluntary exile in the United States. He returned to France after the Restoration. During the years 1816-1822 he was Minister to Washington, though not continuously in residence.

Hyde de Neuville was an energetic and able representative of the Government of France. A man of mercurial temper, he threatened at one time to advise his Government to declare war on the United States. On another occasion he electrified diplomatic circles in Washington when he started to draw his sword against Stratford Canning, the British Minister, after a diplomatic dinner. Nevertheless he was appreciated as a kindly and estimable person. Adams, then Secretary of State, summarized his character: "a mixture of ultra royalism and republican liberality; frank, candid, honorable, generous, benevolent, humane, adoring his country, worshipping Monsieur, the King's brother, and the Duke and Duchess d'Angoulême, adhering upon a principle of honor to his party. . . . He is flighty but not inconstant in his sentiments;

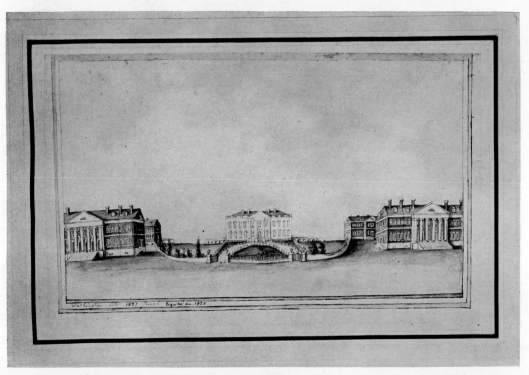

Drawing by Baroness Hyde de Neuville. Probably done from the doorway of Decatur House, depicting the White House in the center, the State, War and Navy Building and the Treasury Building on either side

(Property of the New York Public Library)

THE BENJAMIN OGLE TAYLOE HOUSE ON THE EAST SIDE OF LaFAYETTE SQUARE.
FROM A PAINTING BY FRANCIS C. JONES

accessible to reason, but not powerful as a reasoner; quick but placable in his temper . . . altogether a safe man with whom to transact business."

The Hyde de Neuvilles returned to France temporarily in 1820. President Monroe, wishing him a prosperous voyage, said his return would be anticipated with pleasure, and recalled "with grateful satisfaction the part which France had taken in aid of our Revolution." Adams commented that never before had he heard the President speak with so much feeling to a foreign Minister. The following year Hyde de Neuville returned, having been created a Baron while in France. During his absence the Legation was in charge of M. de Menou, in residence at Decatur House. But this time the Minister's stay was brief, and in 1822 he returned home permanently, to resume his eventful political career.

Now the flags at Decatur House were changed again. It became the Russian Legation, passing to the sovereignty of Czar Alexander. Hyde de Neuville was succeeded at Decatur House by a gentleman with the noteworthy name of Major General Baron Feodor Vasil'evich Teil'-fan-Seroskerken, Russian Minister to the United States. In American circles he was known for convenience as Baron de Tuyll, and in the Congressional Directory for the year 1824 his residence was carefully specified as "Mrs. Decatur's house, north of the President's."

Baron de Tuyll was a gentleman of eminence in Russia. As the name van Seroskerken indicates, he was of Dutch extraction, like a number of the Russian nobility at that time. He had risen to the rank of a major general in the Russian army, and had been accorded the unusual distinction of having an island named after him by a Russian sea captain. As a diplomat he was regarded as a man of great ability. On May 13, 1817, he was appointed Minister to the United States, being also accredited to Portugal and stationed at Rio de Janeiro. After two years of service he was recalled, and was reappointed June 28, 1822, to succeed P. I. Poletika at Washington.

During Baron de Tuyll's second period as Minister, which lasted four years, he lived at Decatur House. While there he was a central figure in one of the greatest diplomatic moves in American history, the promulgation of the Monroe Doctrine. The Doctrine originated as a reaction against the Holy Alliance, a combination of European powers under the guidance of Metternich and the Czar Alexander. At first they sought to include the United States in this international bloc, and the American Government was not initially unsympathetic. But the reactionary policies of the Holy Alliance alienated public opinion in the United States and England. As the Holy Alliance continued to crush popular movements in Europe, it came to be regarded as an instrument of oppression, and aroused much hostility. When George Canning became the British Foreign Minister in 1822 he favored open opposition, and the following year initiated Anglo-American conversations to this end.

"Our Yankee friends," declared Baron de Tuyll, "shrink from European entanglements, but they like to have a finger in every pie." The question of Spanish reconquest of her revolted American colonies touched a sensitive nerve in the United States. Baron de Tuyll, a "kindly and bustling gentleman," visited the White House on November 17, 1823, bringing with him a number of documents concerning Russian views in this matter. One stated that the Czar desired to "guarantee the tranquillity of all the states of which the civilized world is composed." As construed in American circles, this was taken to mean that the Czar was willing to support Spain in reconquest of her colonies. After a cabinet meeting, Secretary of State Adams drafted a tart reply, taking exception to this statement in appropriate diplomatic language, and expressing the aversion of the American Government to the Spanish action in Latin America. Much of the substance of Adams' reply was announced to the world by President Monroe in his Message to Congress, December 2, 1823.

The Monroe Doctrine was received in Europe with hostility. Metternich denounced it as a revolt in itself, as audacious as the American Revolution. Baron de Tuyll, who saw the collapse of his diplomatic maneuvers to obtain American support for the Holy Alliance, urged his Government to register a formal protest. The French Minister also considered such a move, but in the end no protest was made. The Monroe Doctrine became an accepted fact.

Baron de Tuyll accepted his diplomatic defeat philosophically. He continued his quiet course of life at Decatur House, "a prisoner of gout," but that did not discourage his activities as an epicure.

American foods delighted the Baron: "Washington, with its venison, wild turkey, canvasback ducks, oysters and terrapin, furnishes better viands than Paris," he said, "and needs only cooks."

The remainder of his stay was uneventful, except that Mrs. Decatur complained to Henry Clay that the Russian servants were digging up her shrubbery. He returned to Russia when relieved March 3, 1826, and Decatur House resumed its American birthright.

PORTRAIT OF HENRY CLAY, SECRETARY OF STATE,
BY CHARLES B. KING
(In the collection of the Corcoran Gallery of Art, Washington, D. C.)

CHAPTER III

STATESMAN AND ORATOR

HENRY CLAY declared "I would rather be right than be President," but he saw no insuperable obstacle to being both. Clay entered the threshold of Decatur House in the Spring of 1827, with Mrs. Clay, the children and the family baggage. Pending the White House he chose the next closest residence. Of his fifty years, more than twenty-five of them had been spent in public office, and every sign seemed to point to the Presidency as his eventual goal. Now he was Secretary of State, and he lived in symbolic physical proximity to the White House.

In an age of oratory, Henry Clay of Kentucky was the master of them all. His magnificent bearing and magnetic voice swayed the huge crowds that thronged to hear him speak. On these occasions he seemed inspired, and contemporaries likened his voice to a musical instrument that could move his audience at will. In addition, his personality was suffused with a dynamic exuberance that overcame all obstacles. Englishmen fancied a likeness between Clay and the younger Pitt; some observers called him the American Demosthenes. But one thing was certain; as Bancroft said, Henry Clay "did not know how to be dull."

His personal qualities made him a giant in the political scene of his time. To the public he was a beloved figure, who fired the popular imagination with his eloquence. In his political operations he wielded his personal power with obvious zest, to manipulate situations and people as he desired. In his personal contacts he was reckless, sparkling and humorous, a man of irresistible attraction to those about him. John Quincy Adams declared that he had "all the virtues indispensable to a popular man."

As the master of Decatur House, Henry Clay in his private life was courteous and hospitable, as might be expected of a gentleman from Kentucky. He was fond of people and horses; he was known for his entertainments and his thoroughbreds. As all Washington knew, he liked to wager, and was heartily convivial in other ways. But in his home life he was devoted to his wife and his family, and was deeply affected by a series of domestic tragedies. He had six daughters, all of whom died before him; his favorite son was killed in war and another son was left with an impaired mind after an accident.

Henry Clay liked to consider himself of humble birth, but this was a useful exaggeration in politics. He was born in Hanover County, Virginia, in 1777. As a young child, the American Revolution was brought home to him in a literal sense when his father's home was raided by a British cavalry squadron under the command of the notorious Colonel Tarleton. Three years of education in a log schoolhouse were followed by the study of law under the tutelage of Chancellor George Wythe, teacher of Jefferson and Monroe. When he reached the age of twenty he was admitted to the bar at Richmond, and then emigrated to Kentucky, "to grow up with the country." Soon he acquired the reputation of being unequalled as a criminal lawyer. In 1799 he married Lucretia Hart and purchased a home in Kentucky that he named "Ashland."

Clay's meteoric political career began early, and his success was astounding. He was a member of the State Legislature at twenty-six and a United States Senator at twenty-nine. When he entered the House of Representatives in 1811 he was immediately chosen as Speaker, and served there for six consecutive terms.

From the beginning he was an advocate of a strong international policy, which won for him the nickname of "The War Hawk." As the policy he represented led to the War of 1812, it sometimes was called "Mr. Clay's war." At the termination of hostilities he was sent to Ghent to sign the treaty of peace with Great Britain. But he declined President Madison's offer of the post of Minister to Russia, or the Secretaryship of War, as deviations from the evident course of his career. Later he refused an appointment by President Monroe as Minister to England.

In national policy Clay appeared as a champion of the high tariff as a means of promoting the internal development of the country. He was one of the moving spirits behind the tariff bill of 1824, which the Southern states denounced as a "tariff of abominations." Sectional feeling ran high, and in a few years there were ominous mutterings, and open talk of the rights of the several states to nullify the acts of the Federal government. These were the first flashes of lightning that preceded the storm of civil war. In view of this sectional feeling, Clay took the position that the unity of the country required compromise, and he put forward a series of proposals that earned for him the title of "the Great Compromiser." One of the fruits of his devotion to the Union was the great Missouri Compromise of 1820, which attempted to provide a working solution for the growing issue of slavery. It has been said that Clay's genius for compromise helped to postpone the Civil War three times, until the situation eventually passed beyond the possibility of adjustment.

At an early date Clay had become deeply concerned over the efforts of the Latin Americans to achieve their independence. Eighteen millions of people, he declared, were struggling to burst their chains, and as new republics were created, he urged prompt recognition of them. When General Bolívar summoned a Pan-American Congress at Panama, Clay secured the participation of the United States, declaring that the conference would form "a new epoch in human affairs." To this the British Minister, Sir Charles Vaughan, replied: "Perhaps, but there are so many epochs and so many human affairs," a comment that reflected British disinterestedness. The result of the conference was disappointing to Clay; the American delegate arrived too late, and found little had been accomplished. Nevertheless, Clay remained a devoted friend of the Latin American nations, and distinguished himself as an early advocate of the present "Good Neighbor Policy" in the field of Pan-American affairs.

As a party leader of unrivalled popularity, Clay was a logical candidate for the Presidency. He made his first bid in 1824, and was a strong candidate for years in almost every election. On the first occasion his two rivals, Adams and Jackson, forged ahead of him. The popular vote being indecisive, the election went to the House of Representatives. This put the Speaker, Clay, in a decisive position, for he controlled the one crucial vote. He cast the vote for John Quincy Adams, thereby making Adams the next President. Then Adams appointed him Secretary of State.

The immediate results were unfortunate. Jackson's followers attributed the appointment to a corrupt bargain. Clay protested his innocence, but the episode dogged his footsteps for years. In

1826, John Randolph of Roanoke, that extraordinary eccentric, denounced Clay's support of the President, calling it an alliance between Blackleg and Puritan. Promptly Clay called him to account. After the fashion of the times, he challenged Randolph to a duel. Clay, a Kentucky gentleman, was no stranger to duelling, having fought two of them on previous occasions in the course of his political career. This time the duel was held in nearby Virginia. The scene was picturesque but slightly ludicrous; shots were fired but none found their mark, except for a bullet hole through Randolph's overcoat. The two men shook hands. "You owe me a coat, Mr. Clay," said Randolph. "I am glad that the debt is no greater," Clay replied.

The year following the duel, Clay moved into Decatur House. Here there were balls and entertainments galore. Mrs. Clay, wrote Margaret Bayard Smith, was "overwhelmed with company, besides a very large dining company every week and a drawing room every other week. She says when Mr. Clay dines at home, he never dines alone but always has a social company in a family dinner, which however is really the trouble of a large one. She is obliged to go to other people's parties, sick or well, for fear of giving offence."

During the Clays' residence at Decatur House a lurid episode occurred that threw Washington society into a turmoil. In those days Washington had a number of boarding-houses or taverns where transient Congressmen resided. When Senator John Henry Eaton of Tennessee, a close friend of Andrew Jackson, came to Washington in 1818 he found accommodations at one of these places kept by William O'Neale, who sometimes spelled his name O'Neill. Eaton at that time was a wealthy widower of twenty-eight. In the establishment he met the proprietor's daughter, Margaret, an apple-cheeked brunette of twenty-two years, who already had dabbled in romance. After two near-elopements she had become the bride, at twenty, of a Navy purser named John B. Timberlake, whose naval career was handicapped by his sketchy bookkeeping. Senator Eaton found the company of Mrs. Timberlake enchanting, and helped arrange for her husband to take a long sea voyage. But Eaton's relationship with the too-dashing young woman attracted unfavorable notice, and the

President's wife, Mrs. Monroe, informed her that she was not welcome at presidential receptions.

Andrew Jackson arrived in Washington in 1823 as a Senator, and lodged with Eaton at the same establishment. He liked the young woman of the house, and wrote to his wife back home that Mrs. Timberlake entertained "her pious mother with sacred music" every Sunday. When Timberlake himself returned, his bookkeeping unimproved, Eaton posted his bond and obtained for him a place on the *Constitution*, then departing on a four-year cruise. In 1828 Purser Timberlake died on shipboard in the distant Mediterranean, and strange stories circulated in Washington to the effect that he had committed suicide. Actually there is evidence that he died of tuberculosis, a few months after an unsuccessful suicide attempt. In any case, Mrs. Timberlake's allure was not diminished by her widowhood.

That same year Andrew Jackson was elected President, and in choosing his Cabinet he gave the post of Secretary of War to John Henry Eaton, his time-honored friend. There were immediate protests, for this sudden elevation turned a spotlight on Eaton's private life. The obvious solution was for him to marry the now-famous woman. Eaton discussed this course with Jackson, who prodded him strongly to do so. The new President admired and defended Mrs. Timberlake, refusing to credit the gossip against her. About this time Jackson's own wife died, his devoted Rachel. It is possible that Jackson's solicitude for Mrs. Timberlake was prompted in part, at least, by old gossip about his own wife, which had been dug up again in the recent campaign. Jackson blamed this revival of long-dead gossip on Henry Clay, who nearly had to fight another duel.

Eaton married Mrs. Timberlake on January 1, 1829, and the couple opened a large establishment. Mrs. Eaton, now the bona fide wife of a high-ranking official, began leaving her cards. A social storm immediately broke. Most of the ladies of Washington society refused to call on her, though some of the men, with their eye on public office in the new Administration, were less discriminating. Emily Donelson, the niece of Andrew Jackson, who presided over the White House for him, called on Mrs. Eaton once to pacify her uncle, but declared she was so "disgusted" she refused to go again.

Jackson was enraged. He had ignored the protests over Eaton's appointment, remarking that he felt happier in a storm, and in the case of Mrs. Eaton he decided to force the issue. "By the Eternal," he swore, "the spiteful cats who plagued the life out of my patient Rachel shall not scratch this brave little Peggy!" He called on her himself, bringing his nephew, but no lady accompanied them. The wives of the Cabinet members confronted Mrs. Eaton with a wall of stony indifference, and some of the feminine members of the diplomatic corps followed their example. When Jackson invited Mrs. Eaton to dinner, the wives of other Cabinet officials declined. Jackson upbraided their husbands, who pleaded the rule of *place aux dames* in social engagements. "Old Hickory" was now fighting an unfamiliar type of battle; he might defeat the men but the women were a different adversary.

The British Minister, Sir Charles Vaughan, reported the affair thus in a letter home: "The President has made a better impression than his friends feared he might make, but he is likely to get himself in hot water over some of his friendships, particularly of a Quixotic one over a lady who although the wife of one of his Ministers is reputed to be no better than she should be; at all events the wives of the other Ministers will have nothing to do with her. This is causing a vast scandal in Washington, especially as General Jackson has undertaken to champion the lady, making her an honored guest at his dinner parties which in consequence the other women refuse to attend. As Jackson is known to have a hot temper and an unyielding disposition, I foresee a social tempest." Sir Charles was right, at least about the tempest.

The election of Andrew Jackson was a heavy blow to Henry Clay, for Jackson regarded him as a mortal enemy. Clay's tenure as Secretary of State was ended; he would have to return to Kentucky and seek re-election to Congress. Of his role in the Eaton affair it is difficult to be certain. Jackson thought him capable of anything, and blamed him for stirring up stale gossip about Mrs. Jackson, as well as inspiring the vendetta against Mrs. Eaton. But Jackson was an irascible man. Looking back over his life in later years he conceded that he regretted two things: that he had not been able to shoot Henry Clay or hang John C. Calhoun.

With the coming of the Jackson Administration, Washington society was transformed; there was gloom in many homes. A frequent visitor at Decatur House, Maragaret Bayard Smith, wrote that Clay's health was bad; she was "shocked at the alteration of his looks." She lamented other changes as well. "Never before did the city seem to me so gloomy—so many changes in society—so many families broken up, and those of the first distinction. . . . Drawing rooms in which I have so often mixed with gay crowds, distinguished by rank, fashion, beauty, talent . . . now empty, silent, dark, dismantled." So it was with Decatur House, but not for long. Clay and his family departed March 13, 1829, for Kentucky, instead of moving on as he had hoped to the White House.

Another tenant moved into Decatur House, which became involved more than ever in the Eaton case.

M Van Buren

MARTIN VAN BUREN, SECRETARY OF STATE.
ENGRAVED FROM A PHOTOGRAPH
(Johnson Fry & Co., New York)

CHAPTER IV

THE LESSER TALLEYRAND

A GREAT CROWD invaded Washington for Jackson's inaugural. He arrived in the city on the twelfth of February, in Eaton's carriage, and was lodged at Gadsby's. At the same time a hungry horde of office-seekers descended on the city, hopeful of a place in the new Administration. "It was like the inundation of northern barbarians into Rome," someone wrote. The newcomers slept in crowded beds, on billiard tables, and on the floors. There were some 11,000 offices to be had. "To the victor belongs the spoils."

When Jackson selected his Cabinet the top position, that of Secretary of State, was earmarked for Martin Van Buren, then Governor of New York. Van Buren's friends warned him against accepting the post in what they considered a questionable type of Administration. As soon as he arrived in Washington he was besieged by office-seekers. Van Buren left his hotel room to escape them, and made his way to the White House, where he found Jackson tired and ailing. But the new President's eyes brightened when he saw Van Buren, his stalwart friend, who soon became the kingpin of the Administration. Together they revolutionized the political life of the country.

A new regime had come to Decatur House as it had to Washington in general, for now it was the home of the new Secretary of State, Martin Van Buren. As the chief dispenser of political patronage under the new era, as well as the pivotal figure in the Cabinet, he was much sought after by everyone. His home quickly became the political nerve center of the capital. Everyone of importance came there if they could. All Washington knew that there was a signalling device in an attic window of Decatur House, and another in the White House, so that the Secretary and the President could send messages to each other across Lafayette Square. More than one of the messages, no doubt, carried across the intervening grounds the name of Mrs. Eaton.

What Van Buren himself termed "the Eaton malaria" now infected the whole capital; the gossips talked of little else. Jackson himself made it a governmental issue when he called a meeting of his Cabinet and laid before the august gentlemen a mass of evidence designed to vindicate the woman. The evidence, of course, was greeted with crude skepticism. Now the administration of public affairs came to a virtual standstill. The Jackson party regarded the whole matter as a conspiracy against them; the social triumph of Mrs. Eaton was no longer a personal issue; the prestige of the administration was at stake. Never had the nation faced such a preposterous situation. Webster wrote: "It is odd, but the consequences of this desperate turmoil in the social and fashionable world may determine who shall succeed the present Chief Magistrate."

Van Buren himself was well adapted for his share in the imbroglio. Biographers differ in their estimates of him. Sometimes he is described as a crafty mediocrity with a talent for wirepulling and chicanery, a little fellow who richly deserves oblivion. Others have found him a man of sincere convictions, with a record of forceful leadership. But no one denied his aptitude for evasive maneuvering, which John Randolph summarized pointedly: Van Buren "rowed to his object with muffled oars." He took a curious pride in being equivocal, and avoided committing himself. On one occasion, after a forceful speech by Van Buren, an impressed but bewildered listener asked: "Which side is he on?" On another occasion a sporting wager was made on whether he could be forced to take a definite stand. To settle the wager he was asked if the sun rose in the east. He replied that he never got up that early.

With the impartiality of a true strategist Van Buren treated his antagonists with civility and even friendliness. Political enemies, he thought, could remain personally on amiable terms. He had a delightful sense of humor, and his repartee with opponents like Henry Clay and John Randolph provided an endless supply of Washington small talk. For years he shared the snuff and witticisms of his foes. The nicknames they gave him were biting but not malicious: "the Red Fox of Kinderhook," "the Little Magician," "the Lesser Talleyrand."

Van Buren was called the Red Fox of Kinderhook because he had been born in a little town by that name, near Albany, New York. After some scanty education in local schools he became a law clerk at the age of fourteen. From then on he saturated himself with politics, and groomed himself for a public career. At thirty he was a state senator, and four years later, in 1816, he was appointed attorney general of New York. In his home state he acquired the reputation of being a master of intrigue, and his enemies accused him of heartless manipulations. He entered the national scene when elected to the Senate in 1821, and in many senatorial battles demonstrated his political adroitness. Elected Governor of New York in 1828, he resigned a few months later to enter Jackson's Cabinet.

No speaker himself, Van Buren deprecated oratory. The historian Macaulay once declared that "Parliamentary Government is Government by speaking," but Van Buren knew better. He preferred pulling strings to making speeches; he acted while others talked. Not himself a man of ideas, and distrustful of his own intellectual attainments, he liked literary people, and was a friend of Washington Irving, William Cullen Bryant and George Bancroft. In person he was short and erect, with military carriage. Some compared him with Metternich, which no doubt gratified him. This *"fils d'un cabaretier,"* remarked a French Minister, had *"une certaine aisance qui le rend supérieur, comme homme du monde."*

Jackson could scarcely have had a better stage manager for the Eaton affair, which Van Buren handled with the character and methods of a professional politician. Here indeed was an opportunity for the type of maneuvering that he loved. For a newly-elected President the first event on the social schedule was the traditional Cabinet dinner. The prospect of entertaining his official family filled Jackson with alarm; he delayed it for months until Van Buren persuaded him to proceed. At this affair the Cabinet was compelled to meet Mrs. Eaton, but the prevailing atmosphere was glacial. The next event on the official schedule, for which Van Buren made careful preparations, was the Secretary of State's dinner.

In this campaign Van Buren was strategically situated. A widower for some years, he was unrestrained by domestic *convenances,* and could entertain Mrs. Eaton without embarrassment. The son of a tavern-keeper himself, he had no compunctions about welcoming a tavern-keeper's daughter. But the main thing was that Van Buren had his eye on the Presidency; he saw a chance to consolidate his position with Jackson and possibly elbow out a potential rival, Calhoun. Few had many doubts as to his motives; Adams commented acidly that Van Buren was "notoriously engaged in canvassing for the Presidency by paying his court to Mrs. Eaton."

Once more Decatur House was the scene of a memorable occasion. Carriage after carriage brought the guests to the familiar door, and elegantly groomed ladies and gentlemen ascended the curved stairway to the salons above. The air was electric with expectation. Excitement ran high; almost anything was possible. An incident was inevitable, of course, but it proved to be a minor one. The bold Peggy was jostled by the wife of the Chief of Staff, or vice versa. There was a flurry of words, a brief exchange of insults, but no further damage. Van Buren did not witness the episode; he was downstairs getting some punch.

After the entertainment at Decatur House Van Buren felt rather successful, and continued his manipulations. He used the influence of his office to induce two bachelors in the diplomatic corps to be kind to Mrs. Eaton. Apparently not caring to ruffle the Secretary of State, the British and Russian Ministers, Sir Charles Vaughan and Baron Krudener, also entertained in the same way. But this time Van Buren had undertaken too much; his political dexterity was no match for the combined forces of Washington society, and his manipulations merely crystallized the opposition. Even the President's own niece, Mrs. Donelson, defied her uncle and preferred exile to Tennessee rather than accept Mrs. Eaton. Later she returned to the White House.

The situation grew more acute, until finally a serious crisis occurred at a public ball in January, 1830. Here Mrs. Eaton was roundly and effectively insulted, even too much for a tavern-keeper's daughter. For her the end had come. She gave up the struggle and conceded defeat, preferring thereafter to avoid public appearances. The following year her husband was eased out of the

Cabinet, and never again held public office in Washington. Jackson loyally but discreetly found posts for him elsewhere.

The *dénouement* of the affair was delayed for a couple of decades. The ever-faithful Jackson appointed his friend Eaton to be Governor of the territory of Florida, and subsequently Minister to Spain. At the Court of Madrid Mrs. Eaton shone resplendently; there was no animosity to mar her success. Then in 1840 Eaton proved a turncoat; he rewarded Jackson's devotion by going over to Jackson's enemies. In great bitterness the President denounced him as a "degraded apostate." After Eaton died in 1856 his wealthy widow remarried, this time choosing an Italian dancing master. A short time thereafter he decamped with her fortune, and to make the blow complete, eloped with her granddaughter!

All through the complications of the Eaton affair, Martin Van Buren continued to move steadily toward his great goal—the Presidency. But instead of approaching it directly, he preferred a circuitous path. As Davy Crockett said of him, "If he could gain an object as well by openness as intrigue, he would chose the latter." As the virtual Prime Minister and court favorite of the Jackson Administration he was the logical successor to the Presidency, but he preferred more devious tactics. The first step was to resign his Secretaryship so that he could maneuver more freely for the next step, the Vice Presidency. He broached the subject to Jackson one afternoon during a horseback ride, and put the best possible face on it. If he resigned, other Cabinet members would follow his example, and Jackson would have the opportunity to renovate the Cabinet. And so it was arranged. As a fitting reward for his apparent self-sacrifice, Van Buren was appointed Minister to England, and had the virtual assurance of second place on the party ticket for the next election.

Van Buren set out for London carrying a Minister's portfolio, and made an extraordinarily good impression at the Court of St. James. A courtier by instinct, he fitted into the situation with tact and grace, charming the King and Queen as well as others. One day a letter from home brought him the news that the Senate had failed to confirm his appointment:

Washington, 27 Jan'y, 1832

"My dear friend:

I most sincerely congratulate you on your rejection by the Senate—23 to 23 and by the casting vote of the Vice President. . . . I consider this as a providential interposition in your favor. . . . The thing is admirable—you will be our Vice President."

Van Buren received the news with unconcealed delight. He was not the Minister to England, after all. But he was something else which he considered more important. His enemies had fallen into a masterful ambush. By blocking the Administration's gift of the Ministry, they ensured that Van Buren would receive another gift he valued more.

Jackson was re-elected in 1832, with Van Buren as his Vice President instead of Calhoun. Now the path was clear for the Red Fox of Kinderhook; he knew he would be the next President. It was not necessary to maneuver any further; he could relax and let events take their course. But there were clouds on the horizon. The country was restless and unsettled; "society seems everywhere unhinged," declared a contemporary account. There was a general fear of open violence, and Clay ominously referred to the era as a "hitherto bloodless" revolution. The country was presented with the remarkable picture of Van Buren presiding over the Senate with a brace of pistols in his belt.

Of the two residents of Decatur House who yearned to be President, Clay and Van Buren, one failed and the other succeeded. Van Buren was elected in 1836 as the eighth President of the United States. But he was the inheritor of disaster. A financial panic swept the country, and his political skill was useless. His drifting policy did nothing to bring relief; day by day his popularity ebbed. For the next election the Whigs nominated a popular military hero, William Henry Harrison, to oppose Van Buren. During the campaign Harrison was pictured as a Man of the People, and his platform consisted mainly of coonskins, log cabins and hard cider. Van Buren was accused of eating from gold plates and putting cologne on his whiskers. The outcome was a crushing defeat for the Red Fox of Kinderhook, by an electoral vote of 234 to 60.

The Lesser Talleyrand

It is a curious paradox that a man like Van Buren, who had held so many high offices, was not a success in his own eyes. This was because he left the White House in an utter rout, playing the role of a "martyred exile." He failed in three subsequent campaigns to regain the Presidency.

Van Buren finally realized that he was politically a deceased character, says a recent biographer. "He would not be buried for fourteen years thereafter, but, remaining above ground, it was only to know the appalling experience of viewing his own remains, of seeing himself as posterity would see him. He was seventeen when he tried for his first public trust and sixty-six when he tried for his last one. Over that half-century there had been several times when he was not holding a political office, but none when he was not a candidate for one. Until beaten by Harrison, he never experienced a major setback.

"By all laws of logic and arithmetic, Martin Van Burren knew he should rank with the greatest of statesmen, but the irrefutable fact stared him in the face that he did not. . . . It is well that he lived no longer than he did. Happy for him that he never knew how his family, his village, his state, his country, would neglect not only his fame but his memory.

"His State, from which he was the first President, recalled the fact only in 1910, when Governor Charles Evans Hughes vetoed a bill to build him a monument. And as for his countrymen— when in 1934 a batch of presidential signatures went up for auction, his brought $2.25—which was $1.75 less than Polk's."

Engraved by E. Wellmore from a Drawing by J. B. Longacre.

EDWARD LIVINGSTON.

Edw Livingston

EDWARD LIVINGSTON, SECRETARY OF STATE.
ENGRAVED FROM A DRAWING
(James B. Longacre)

CHAPTER V

THE LIVINGSTONS

DECATUR HOUSE was alight with wedding festivities in the year 1833, celebrations for the famous belle of the Jackson era, Cora Livingston, whom enthusiastic contemporaries called "the queen of American society." Her proud and happy father, Edward Livingston, had leased Decatur House two years before as a Washington residence for the family while he served as Secretary of State under President Jackson. Here the Livingstons dispensed their lavish hospitality, culminating in the marriage of their daughter, Cora, to Thomas P. Barton, of Philadelphia. There had been no happier event in the rich and varied history of Decatur House.

Only a few months before, in this same house, Edward Livingston had left his own mark on American history. As Secretary of State, the eminent jurist had been called upon by President Jackson to act in a great crisis confronting the nation. The grim issue of secession had been raised by South Carolina, which in 1832 nullified Federal laws and threatened to organize a separate government. Faced with this challenge, Jackson acted with decision. To Livingston he entrusted the task of drafting a proclamation to the nation, reasserting the nature of the Union and denying to the states the right to secede. At Decatur House Livingston began work at once, drawing up a new declaration of constitutional principles. Page by page, as he finished writing, the document was rushed to the White House, where it was issued over the President's signature on December 10, 1832.

Livingston's masterly proclamation created a sensation. The country, he declared, was a national unit, over and above the several states. If the Federal Government overstepped its powers, it was the task of the judiciary to curb it, not the states themselves. Secession, he declared, was revolution. These ringing principles surprised the North and South alike; the Administration found them "equally confounding to friend and foe." Van Buren thought the proclamation went too far. Adams called it "a blister plaster." Calhoun feared it meant a miltary despotism. South Carolina protested. But its purpose was accomplished, and the trend toward nullification was checked. Eventually, after an armed struggle, the national conception expressed by Livingston prevailed.

Jackson was fortunate in having, at this juncture, a Secretary of State with such eminent qualifications as Edward Livingston. In the Spring of 1831 the Cabinet conflict precipitated by the Eaton affair had been resolved by a stratagem conceived by the Red Fox of Kinderhook. Van Buren and Eaton resigned at the same time, giving Jackson an excuse to reshuffle his Cabinet. It was decided to appoint a man of highest calibre as Secretary of State, and the choice fell to Livingston. He hesitated and asked time to consider, but Jackson was insistent. The result was that Livingston succeeded Van Buren both as Secretary of State and as master of Decatur House.

Of patrican parentage, the son of a famous Revolutionary War patriot, Edward Livingston was born in 1764 at his family's home "Clermont" in New York. His early life was pervaded by the tumultuous atmosphere of the Revolutionary period, but this did not prevent him from attending the College of New Jersey (Princeton), from which he was graduated in 1781. He began law studies at Albany, in the office of John Lansing, where his fellow students were Alexander Hamilton and Aaron Burr. After the British evacuated New York in 1783, Livingston and his family moved there, and he was admitted to the bar. Immediately he benefitted from the ample litigation that the British occupation had produced.

It was not long before "Beau Ned," as young Livingston was called, became a figure of prominence in New York society. In due course he was attracted to the three daughters of Charles McEvers, a merchant of the city. Their charms he commemorated in a bit of verse, inscribed on the flyleaf of his copy of Longinus:

> Longinus, give thy lessons o'er;
>   I do not need thy rules:
> Let pedants on thy precepts pore,
>   Or give them to the schools.

Miss Cora Livingston, daughter of Edward Livingston.
From a miniature by herself

The Livingstons

> The perfect beauty which you seek,
>   In Anna's verse I find;
> It glows on fair Eliza's cheek,
>   And dwells in Mary's mind.

Apparently the beauty of verse and cheek appealed to him less than beauty of the mind, for he chose the eldest daughter, Mary, and they were married in 1788. She died some years later during an epidemic of scarlet fever.

His political career began at the age of thirty, when he was elected to Congress. There he led the opposition to Jay's Treaty, and fought against the Alien and Sedition Law. After he declined to run again he was appointed District Attorney for New York, and the same year became Mayor of the city. Then the beginnings of a brilliant career were blighted by tragic circumstances. An epidemic of fever that swept New York in 1803 was no respecter of persons; even the mayor contracted the disease and was critically ill. Upon his recovery he found another disaster had struck. One of his confidential clerks had mismanaged or misused Custom House funds for which Livingston was responsible. At once he resigned from office and surrendered all his personal property to cover the loss. This being inadequate, he willingly assumed a crushing burden of debt for the remainder. His career seemed terminated in utter ruin.

With great fortitude, however, Livingston decided upon a fresh start amid new surroundings. The vast Louisiana territory had just been purchased from France, largely through the efforts of his elder brother, Chancellor Livingston, then Minister at Paris. The same year, 1803, Edward Livingston set out for New Orleans, with only a hundred dollars in gold and a letter of credit for a thousand more. An able linguist, he was immediately at home in the French-speaking city. He resumed legal practice, was very successful, and before long became one of the leading citizens of New Orleans. In 1805 he married a beautiful young widow, Louise de Lassy, of a French family from Santo Domingo. Their daughter, Cora, was born during an eclipse the following year, and Livingston wrote: "God has given me so fair a daughter that the sun has hidden his face."

In the War of 1812 he helped to mobilize resistance against the British, as the city's Chairman of Public Defense, and obtained amnesty for the notorious pirate Lafitte in return for military assistance. To General Jackson he transmitted maps and military information, and welcomed the general to New Orleans in 1814. This was the beginning of a lifelong friendship between the two. He remained Jackson's aide-de-camp and interpreter until the war ended.

Long and complicated litigation occupied Livingston after the war, and he was elected to the Louisiana legislature. There an opportunity presented itself that was to make him internationally famous. In 1821 he was appointed to prepare a complete revision of the penal code. This was a monumental undertaking, for the laws of Louisiana were a curious mixture from Roman, Spanish and French sources. Trial by jury and other features of English common law were recent innovations. Livingston's task was to remove the contradictions and reconcile these different legal systems, at the same time introducing certain much-needed reforms. He labored for two years at this task, and completed an exhaustive system of penal law, but the manuscript of his work was destroyed by fire. Undaunted, he spent two more years in reproducing the work, which was finally published and attracted worldwide attention. The "Livingston Code," which made him famous, was humane in spirit rather than vindictive, and abolished capital punishment.

The reception of his work was all that he could ask, though it was not adopted by his state. It was immediately reprinted in England, France and Germany, and had a wide influence on penal legislation. Victor Hugo wrote: "You will be numbered among the men of this age who have deserved the most and best of mankind." A more authoritative tribute came from the great jurist Sir Henry Maine, who described Livingston as "the first legal genius of modern times."

Meanwhile his abiding interest in politics continued, and in 1822 he was elected to the House of Representatives for the first of three terms. At about the same time his friend Jackson also went to Washington as Senator. In the House, Livingston's career crossed the same path that it had reached many years before. Finally in

1826 he paid off the last of his debt to the Government incurred nearly a quarter of a century before. The havoc of his early years was more than repaired. He became a Senator in 1829, as Jackson moved on to the Presidency.

In Washington circles he was known as "a charming, scholarly gentleman, devoted to literature, historical research, legal reform, and his lovely wife." Those looking for faults found them, if at all, in his "kindly nature and easy credulity." Jackson himself summarized his character from the viewpoint of a border captain: "A polished scholar, an able writer, and a most excellent man," though Jackson could not help adding, "He knows nothing of mankind."

It was natural that Jackson would offer him an important post, which was that of Minister to France, but Livingston's private affairs prevented his acceptance. In 1831, he decided to retire. Upon his sister's death a few years before, Livingston had inherited a country estate on the Hudson called "Montgomery Place," in Dutchess County. This now became his home, where he expected to spend his remaining years. But very shortly he received an urgent letter from the Secretary of State, Martin Van Buren, requesting his immediate presence in Washington. There he learned that Jackson was dissolving his Cabinet, and had decided that Livingston would succeed Van Buren as Secretary of State.

Thus Livingston emerged from his brief retirement to accept the appointment. A month later he wrote his wife: "Here I am in the second place in the United States,—some say the first; in the place filled by Jefferson and Madison and Monroe, and by him who filled it before any of them,—my brother; in the place gained by Clay at so great a sacrifice; in the very easy chair of Adams; in the office which every politician looks to as the last step but one in the ladder of his ambition; in the very cell where the Great Magician, they say, brewed his spells. Here I am without an effort, uncontrolled by any engagements, unfettered by any promise to party or to man."

When, as Secretary of State, Livingston took up his residence in Decatur House, he was nearly seventy, a tall, slight figure of a man, with a bold forehead and peaceful dark eyes. His biographer, Hunt, writes: "His manner of living and of entertaining guests was not excelled in elegance, if equalled, in Washington. In this his wife saved him all manner of exertion. No woman could be better qualified to preside in such a house than she. Having possessed striking beauty while young, and still retaining very remarkable dignity and grace, her mind was as extraordinary as her manners and person. Unacquainted with the English language before her marriage to Mr. Livingston, she had learned it mainly out of the English classics, and, though she always continued to speak it with a marked accent, had acquired a complete mastery of diction." When Livingston often turned to her for counsel, she compared her role with amusement to the serving-girl to whom Molière read his comedies.

Brilliantly completing the household was their daughter, Cora, of whom Josiah Quincy wrote: "Burke's famous apostrophe to the Queen of France is none too good for the queen of American society." The same year of her marriage, in 1833, Livingston was appointed Minister to France, and his son-in-law, Barton, became Secretary of Legation.

Edward Livingston spent the next two years in France deeply occupied with negotiations over American claims arising from French spoliations of American shipping. In an interval of strained relations he was directed to close the negotiations and return home. He died a few months later at his home on the Hudson.

SIR CHARLES VAUGHAN,
BRITISH MINISTER TO THE UNITED STATES

CHAPTER VI

THE BRITISH MINISTER

IN 1835 HARRIET MARTINEAU visited the city, with her silver ear trumpet much in evidence. "The city," she wrote, "is unlike any other that ever was seen, straggling out hither and thither, with a small house or two a quarter of a mile from any other, so that in making calls 'in the city' we had to cross ditches and stiles, and walk alternately on grass and pavements, and strike across a field to reach a street. . . . Then there was the society, singularly compounded from the largest variety of elements; foreign Ambassadors, the American government, members of Congress, from Clay and Webster down to Davy Crockett, Benton from Missouri, and Cuthbert, with the freshest Irish brogue, from Georgia; flippant young belles, pious wives dutifully attending their husbands, and groaning over the frivolities of the place; grave judges, saucy travelers, pert newspaper reporters, melancholy Indian chiefs, and timid New England ladies, trembling on the verge of the vortex; all this was wholly unlike anything that is to be seen in any other city in the world; for all these are mixed up together in daily intercourse like the higher circle of a little village."

By now La Fayette Square, surrounded by famous houses, was in its full glory as the center of political and social happenings in Washington. An "elegant" new brick house was built there about 1835, on what is now Madison Place, by Commodore John Rodgers, a hero of the Tripoli War, who in his later years was called "the Nestor of the Navy." According to rumor the lot on which the house was built had been acquired from Henry Clay, who exchanged it for an Andalusian jackass that the Commodore had brought back from the Mediterranean. Clay himself had obtained the piece of ground one evening when the cards were favorable, and was happy to part with it for a valuable animal for his Kentucky stud-farm, where for years it was known as "the braying grandfather of La Fayette Square."

43

Decatur House again became a center of diplomatic life as the residence of the British Minister to the United States, Sir Charles Richard Vaughan. He had come to America first in 1825, as the successor of Stratford Canning, and had acquired the reputation of being a charming and able diplomat. "Few men," says Willson, "had a wider acquaintance with the forms and secrets of diplomacy." Combined with this was an unusually piquant personality, that provided the source of many anecdotes. Believing that in a republic he should act with appropriate *bonhomie,* he peppered his conversation with slang and even profanity. On one occasion, when a guest remarked about the warm weather, he replied, "Warm, madam! It's as hot as hell!"

Sir Charles was a man of cosmopolitan tastes and training, acquired in the course of a long diplomatic career. Born in 1774, he had been educated at Rugby and Oxford, and took his degree in medicine. But his intention of becoming a physician was quickly altered. In 1800 he was appointed by the university to a travelling fellowship, and spent the next three years on the Continent, visiting various countries. Thus acquiring a taste for foreign travel, he arranged another trip to Asia Minor, including a journey from Aleppo to Bagdad. Falling ill in Persia, he was aided by some Russian officers, and upon his recovery accompanied them to the Volga. Shut in by ice, he spent a winter on the deserted island of Kulali before returning to St. Petersburg and London.

His real life work began in 1808, when he was offered a diplomatic post and accompanied Sir Charles Stuart to Spain. In that war-torn country he witnessed much fighting around Madrid and Saragossa, and wrote an account of it for English readers. His book, *The Narrative of the Siege of Saragossa,* was published upon his return, and attracted much attention. He became private secretary to the British Foreign Secretary, Lord Bathurst.

Sir Charles subsequently moved on to a succession of diplomatic posts. He was appointed Secretary of Legation in Madrid, and became Acting Minister in 1815-16. This was followed by an interval at Paris as Secretary of the Embassy under his friend Sir Charles Stuart, after which he became Minister to the Confederated States of Switzerland. In 1825 he was appointed Minister to the United States.

Arriving at Annapolis in August, he proceeded to Washington and arrived in time to witness the departure of the aged Marquis de La Fayette, who had made an historic tour of the country and was returning to France. Taking up his ministerial duties, Sir Charles called upon President John Quincy Adams, who did not hesitate to express his chagrin over "the humiliating circumstances of his election." Another call was upon Henry Clay, the new Secretary of State, who was smarting under the charges of a "corrupt bargain" behind his appointment. From now on, Sir Charles was an observer of an interesting period in American history, notable for party strife for the control of the government.

Sir Charles' love of travel reasserted itself, and in a new country he could not resist the temptation to explore its vast domains. He found occasion to make two long tours that carried him to the most remote places. His ministerial affairs were not too exacting, but covered a wide range of problems, among them the Canadian boundary question, the suppression of the slave trade, American policy toward the Latin American republics, and the never-ending tariff details. He also participated slightly in a more intimate aspect of American life when he entertained, on one occasion, a wayward young woman named Peggy Eaton.

Sir Charles Vaughan succeeded the Livingstons at Decatur House in 1834, and resided there until he finally left Washington in October, 1835. Upon his departure, Decatur House was acquired by another type of occupant.

CHAPTER VII

THE GADSBY INTERVAL

EW HAPPENINGS at Decatur House escaped the watchful eyes
of Benjamin Ogle Tayloe, who recorded them from time to
time in his memoirs. "On Sir Charles Vaughan leaving the
Decatur House," he noted, "it passed into the possession of
mine host of the *National*, Mr. John Gadsby." This was in 1836,
when Gadsby purchased the house for $12,000, and invaded the
select circles of Washington society.

The new occupant of Decatur House represented another phase
of Washington life, neither war, diplomacy nor politics, but a new
mercantile class then appearing in the city. There was no industrial
development in Washington, and therefore no class of industrial
tycoons. Gadsby's success was as the proprietor of famous hotels
and taverns in Alexandria, Baltimore and Washington. At the
National Hotel in Washington he was host to countless eminent
personages of his time. In the course of his career he had entertained
every President since George Washington, and his name was a
byword among the many historical figures who came to the national
capital; it is estimated that five hundred of them mentioned him
in their correspondence.

By training Gadsby was a builder, if not an architect. There
are many uncertainties about his early life, but he was born in
London in 1766, and was educated there. After the American
Revolution he crossed the Atlantic, some time before 1792, and
became a resident of Alexandria, Virginia. It is possible that he
designed the City Tavern in Alexandria, one of the best-known
hostelries of the time, which he afterwards operated. In any case
an English traveler in America, Richard Parkinson, commented in
the year 1798: "Mr. Gadsby, the landlord, is an Englishman from
London," and added that he "was a builder by profession."

He became landlord in a very simple way. The first proprietor
of the "City Tavern, Sign of the Bunch of Grapes," was John
Wise, who apparently failed in business and his creditors took over.

By this means Gadsby acquired the hotel and a new role in life, that of Boniface to the weary traveler. In 1797 he welcomed General Washington on his triumphal return from Philadelphia to Mount Vernon. The General was greeted with a great celebration and much speechmaking, followed by a state dinner at Gadsby's Tavern, as it came to be known.

The vicissitudes of a tavern-keeper's life were evident on this occasion. In the general excitement of the evening some of the guests apparently overlooked the detail of paying their bill. Accordingly, as a polite reminder, Gadsby advertised in the Alexandria paper: "Please call and leave your names at the bar, you gentlemen who dined at the entertainment given Gen. Washington, and had not previously procured tickets." The advertisement added pointedly that he was obliged to take this step, "as from the hurry of business during the day, it was impossible to ascertain the names of all the gentlemen who attended."

It was not long before his business talents became very evident. To obtain a steady flow of customers he organized a new stagecoach line to link his establishment with similar places in Winchester, York, Lancaster and Philadelphia. Now Gadsby could guarantee the traveler a speedy trip from Alexandria to Philadelphia in four days, in good English stagecoaches, that departed and arrived on a reliable schedule. As the terminus of such a line, Gadsby's Tavern was soon the mecca of incoming and outgoing travelers.

In other ways, too, the tavern became a focal point in the social life of the city. When the Alexandria Theatre was organized in 1797 its headquarters were in Gadsby's Tavern, and its ticket office was the bar. The actors also played at Richmond, Petersburg and Norfolk, probably the first theatrical circuit in America. While in Alexandria they stayed at Gadsby's, where occasionally they disported themselves sufficiently to cause comment. A guest at this time wrote: "About half past eight the . . . players came in in a body. They had been at a 'drinking party' in the neighborhood. Once, in Virginia, these drinking parties were called 'barbecues.' Now they say at once a 'drinking party.'" These observations were jotted down by Benjamin Latrobe, himself the first professional architect in America. He added that the players rapidly became a "drunken party."

JOHN GADSBY. FROM A PAINTING BY JOHN GADSBY CHAPMAN;
HANGS IN GADSBY'S TAVERN, ALEXANDRIA, VIRGINIA

PROVIDENCE NORRIS GADSBY, WIFE OF JOHN GADSBY. FROM
A PAINTING BY JOHN GADSBY CHAPMAN; HANGS IN
GADSBY'S TAVERN, ALEXANDRIA, VIRGINIA

There were many other activities at a public tavern in those days. Here at Gadsby's there were weekly dances conducted by the Alexandria Dancing Assembly—tickets $8.00 a season. Trustees of various organizations held business meetings at the tavern. Here George Washington presided over the trustees' meetings of the Powtomack Company, which he had organized to promote navigation on the Potomac River. At one of these meetings he arranged for the company to employ a chief engineer, who was none other than James Rumsey, the man who built one of the first steamboats in America.

On Washington's fiftieth birthday a ball was given in his honor at Gadsby's. "Went up to Alexandria to the celebration of my birthday," wrote Washington in 1799. "Many manoeuvers were performed by the uniform corps, and an elegant ball and supper at night." The ball was a great success, and the custom of having "Birth-Night Balls" on Washington's birthday was continued. This was only one of many times when Washington was entertained at Gadsby's Tavern. The menu for his last meal there has been preserved, a luncheon of "canvasback ducks in a chafing dish, some hominy and old Madeira wine."

When the growth of the town of Alexandria lagged behind the expansion of Philadelphia, Baltimore and Washington, Gadsby decided to leave for greener pastures. After some time in Philadelphia he moved to Baltimore and became proprietor of the Indian Queen Tavern. He installed running water in the tavern, then a true novelty, and made it one of the leading establishments in the country. According to a Baltimore paper, "It is well known that he is the first man who introduced the proper style and taste for public entertainments in this city." In the early 1820's he sold the Indian Queen and moved to Washington.

The story is that Senator John Eaton persuaded him to try his talents in the national capital. Gadsby purchased the Franklin House, which had been operated by Peggy O'Neale's father, at Nineteenth and I Streets. Gadsby remodeled the place and renamed it Gadsby's Tavern. On La Fayette's last visit to America in 1824, President Monroe wished to have him as a guest in the White House, but, instead, the District government installed La Fayette in Gadsby's Tavern. Here a state dinner was given in honor of the distinguished visitor, and the President and many other notables were present.

Gadsby was not entirely satisfied with the location of his establishment, because it was too far from the Capitol. He provided coaches for the Congressmen to ride back and forth, but made plans for a more conveniently situated hotel. At the corner of Pennsylvania Avenue and 6th Street were some vacant lots, owned by the Calvert family, and Gadsby entered into a partnership to build a new hotel on this site. Here the National Hotel was constructed, and when it was opened in 1827 Gadsby boasted that it was the first building in the United States to be designed for hotel purposes. In his eyes, also, it was the largest and best.

For its day, it was a sumptuous establishment, and Gadsby operated it accordingly. "He conducted it in a sort of military style," wrote Nathan Sargent in his book *Public Men and Events*, "and especially was this observed at his long dinner table. The guests being all seated, and an army of colored servants standing behind the chairs, Mr. Gadsby, a short, stout gentleman, standing at the head of the table, the guests silent with expectation, the word was given, 'Remove covers!' when all the servants moved like automata, each at the same moment placing his hand upon the handle of a cover, each at the same time lifting it, stepping back in line and facing the head of the table, and, at a sign from Mr. Gadsby, all marching and keeping regular step to the place of depositing the covers, and then back, to commence waiting on the guests."

"Who of the hundreds of thousands," continued the same writer, "who in these good old cheap times—only $1.25 a day—enjoyed the hospitalities of this gentlemanly and most liberal Boniface, can forget his urbane manner, his careful attention to his guests, his well-ordered house, his fine old wines and the princely manner in which he would send his bottle of choice Madeira to some old friend or favored guest at the table?"

While the hotel was being built, Gadsby purchased the Decatur House, just vacated by the British Minister, Sir Charles Vaughan. By this time he was reputed to be the wealthiest man in Washington, and he and his wife lived in what was then considered a semiregal manner. As a specialist in the art of entertaining, Gadsby gave parties that were unsurpassed. To Washington society he was a new and intriguing type. Statesmen, diplomats and social leaders continued to flock to his door, because they were accustomed to going to Decatur House and because Gadsby knew how to entertain them. However, he was accepted with some pointed qualifications. As one diplomat commented, *"Je sais que c'est un cochon, mais j'y vais quand même."*

Another impression of Gadsby's parties was recorded by the French Minister, the Chevalier Adolphe de Bacourt. "Some days ago I went to an evening party at Mr. Gadsby's, proprietor of the hotel where I stayed on my arrival here. He is an old wretch who has made a fortune in the slave trade, which does not prevent Washington society from rushing to his house, and I should make my government very unpopular if I refused to associate with this kind of people. This gentleman's house is the most beautiful in the city, very well furnished, and perfect in the distribution of the rooms, but the society, my God!"

It was true that Gadsby dabbled in the slave trade, and conducted slave auctions in the walled enclosure behind the house. In the course of this business he occasionally kept some of them in the servants' quarters. "At night," said a contemporary, "you could hear their howls and cries," though this seems like a fanciful exaggeration. It was also believed that he shipped large numbers of slaves to Georgia, for work on the cotton plantations. Thus was another chapter added to the varied history of Decatur House, still less than twenty years old.

By this time the city of Washington was growing rapidly, with a population of 44,000 in 1840, as against 14,000 in 1800. The pattern of social life was perceptibly changing; many more private residences were being built, and Congressmen who formerly lived in boarding houses now came to Washington with their families, who took part in the city's social life. But the city's straggling appearance still invited the witticisms of travelers. "Everybody knows that Washington has a Capitol," wrote Captain Marryat in 1838, "but the misfortune is that the Capitol wants a city. There it stands, reminding you of a general without an army." Four years later Charles Dickens visited the city on his American tour, and said it consisted of "spacious avenues that begin in nothing and lead nowhere; streets a mile long that only want houses, roads, and inhabitants; public buildings that need but a public to be complete; and ornaments of great thoroughfares which only need great thoroughfares to ornament." He added: "One might fancy the season over, and most of the houses gone out of town with their masters."

With the passing years La Fayette Square witnessed the usual parade of personages and events. After President Madison died in 1836 his widow moved into the house on the Square built by her brother-in-law Richard Cutts, and still known as the Dolly Madison House. There she received the homage of all circles of Washington society until her death twelve years later. At the corner of the Square, where Madison Place meets Pennsylvania Avenue, lived the well-known dentist Dr. James S. Gunnell, who received a call one morning from the White House. Putting some instruments into a case, he hurried across the street to treat his patient, President Van Buren. After a brief interval, he emerged from the White House as Postmaster of Washington.

John Gadsby, tavern-keeper extraordinary, died on May 15, 1844, and was buried in the Congressional Cemetery. Decatur House was inherited by his wife, who leased it to a succession of occupants.

George Mifflin Dallas,
Vice President of the United States

CHAPTER VIII

THE VICE PRESIDENT

I
N THE Chamber of the Supreme Court a group of prominent men gathered around a newly-installed electrical device. The machine clattered abruptly, and spelled out the words:

WHAT HATH GOD WROUGHT? . . . . HAVE YOU ANY NEWS? . . . . NO . . . . SEPARATE YOUR WORDS MORE . . . . OIL YOUR CLOCKWORK.

It was May 24, 1844, and this was the first telegraph machine, in operation between Washington and Baltimore. After the initial pious exclamation the first message was a request for news, which was not long in forthcoming. In Baltimore the Democratic convention was in session, to pick the party's presidential candidates for the next election. Martin Van Buren was the leading candidate, and seemed assured of the nomination. The telegraph machine essayed a political joke:

VAN BUREN CANNON IN FRONT, WITH A FOXTAIL ON IT.

The Red Fox of Kinderhook was having trouble, however. On the first ballot he received a majority of votes, but the total was short of the required two-thirds. As the balloting continued the convention was deadlocked by Southern opposition to Van Buren, and a compromise candidate was chosen. Over the telegraph came news of the nomination of James K. Polk, of Tennessee, for the presidency, and the selection of his running mate, who was George Mifflin Dallas, of Pennsylvania.

After the nomination some newspapers inquired sarcastically, "Who is James K. Polk?" Dallas, however, was a prominent figure in the political scene; he had been American Minister to Russia, and prior to that a Senator and attorney general of Pennsylvania. Polk and Dallas were opposed by Henry Clay, running on the Whig ticket and perennially hopeful of the presidency. But fate was against him; in the ensuing election Polk and Dallas were elected by a small majority.

When Dallas came to Washington he needed a residence appropriate for his position as Vice President, and accordingly leased Decatur House from Gadsby's widow. He immediately restored the character and atmosphere of the house, for Dallas was a gentleman of the old school, personifying the best traditions in American life. Washington society found him charming; his wife and childred fitted into the picture equally well. During their residency Decatur House resumed its birthright as an inner sanctum of the city's social life.

By this time La Fayette Square was well built up, and had assumed its ultimate form as a city park, surrounded by the homes of statesmen, diplomats, and people of wealth and fashion. It was also a congregating place for office-seekers and others who desired an audience with the President, whereupon it was christened the "lobby of the White House." Through its winding paths continued to walk, at one time or another, all the great and near-great figures of American life, men who were concerned intimately or remotely with the history of the nation.

No sooner had the new Administration taken office than it found itself on the verge of war. The annexation of Texas in 1845 precipitated a clash with Mexico, and the following year President Polk ordered troops to the Rio Grande. As Vice President, Dallas presided over the Senate during this difficult period. From his previous experience he was well qualified for this position, and played an effective role in the guidance of national policy toward the great goal of the winning of the West.

George M. Dallas was a product of the distinctive social environment of late eighteenth-century Philadelphia. Born in 1792, he was the son of Alexander J. Dallas, Secretary of the Treasury under Madison. He began the study of law in his father's office, and when Albert Gallatin went to Russia in 1813 he took young Dallas along as his personal secretary. The young man returned the following year as a courier bearing the text of the treaty that ended the War of 1812. In Washington he entered the Treasury Department, then under his father's guidance, and soon afterwards was appointed counsel for the Second Bank of the United States. But politics exercised an irresistible fascination, and he attached himself to the Jackson party. After holding some minor offices, he was elected to the Senate in 1831. But there he was in an awkward position, for he was at odds with Jackson on the Bank question, and after one term he retired to private law practice.

Immediately he was appointed attorney general of Pennsylvania, and four years later, in 1837, he was chosen by President Van Buren to represent the United States at the Court of the Czar. During his stay in Russia he kept a vivid diary of his experiences in the court life of the old regime. Among his ministerial duties were negotiations over American rights in the north Pacific, which had to be made safe for American shipping. After a successful performance of these duties, he returned to the United States to re-enter the political field, and became Vice-President in 1844.

The country was now moving closer to the inevitable conflict. Acquisition of new Western territories raised the problem of the extension of slavery, thus intensifying sectional antagonism. Political feeling became intense in the North as well as the South. President Polk tried ineffectually to moderate the furore, and denounced those who raised the slavery issue. "The agitation of the slavery question," he declared, "is mischievous and wicked," and he added that it had "no legitimate connection with the War with Mexico." Under pressure from all sides, he took his stand: "I put my face alike against Southern agitators and Northern fanatics." Consequently each side accused him of favoring the other, a natural assumption under the circumstances. Instead of quelling the storm, he merely brought down wrath on his own head. At the Democratic convention in 1848 Polk and Dallas were not renominated. General Zachary Taylor, hero of the Mexican War, was elected.

Just before the election, there was a burst of electrifying news that set the world agog with excitement. On September 16, 1848, a naval courier reached Washington with the news that gold had been discovered in California. The courier, Lieutenant Edward F. Beale, arrived after a fabulous 4,000-mile journey overland across Mexico, his saddlebags stuffed with dispatches, and carrying a small bottle of gold dust and some nuggets. He told his story to a spellbound Senate; how the discovery had been made near Sacramento, and the wild rush that began when a San Francisco newspaper printed the news. He had been dispatched at once to carry word of the discovery to Washington, and arrived after a record-breaking journey. President Polk reported the epochal event to the nation in an official message. From all parts of America, and indeed from all parts of the world, hopeful men set out for California.

It was some while before Washington quieted down. In the meantime George M. Dallas left the Vice-Presidency and retired briefly from public life. Then President Pierce in 1856 appointed him Minister to Great Britain, and he held this key position for five years during the critical period pending the outbreak of the Civil War. He returned home on the eve of hostilities, thus escaping the burden of wartime negotiations that devolved upon his successor. He died three years later, at the age of seventy-two. The city of Dallas, Texas, which was founded in 1841, was named in his honor.

Following Dallas, a succession of tenants occupied Decatur House. Mr. Tayloe noted in his memoirs that "apartments in the second and third stories were rented, first to Mr. Gales, who always entertained handsomely, and for two winters to Messrs. John A. and James G. King, sons of the distinguished Rufus King, and members of the House from New York and New Jersey."

These partial tenants of Decatur House were interesting gentlemen and worthy occupants of the historic mansion. The Mr. Gales who "entertained handsomely" had been mayor of Washington from 1827 to 1830. An Englishman by birth and a journalist by profession, he had come to America as a child in the company of his father, whose acid comments on the Pitt regime had forced him to seek refuge. Joseph Gales learned journalism from his father, and at the age of twenty-one moved to Washington to report Congressional affairs for the *National Intelligencer,* a newspaper known as the official or "Court paper." At first he was the only journalist covering the Senate sessions, and sat beside the presiding officer, sharing his snuff box. Being very successful, Gales purchased the *Intelligencer* in 1810. A private in the Army during the War of 1812, Gales continued to publish the paper with the assistance of his partner, William W. Seaton, until the British captured the city and burned his equipment. He prospered again after the war, and became a prominent figure in the city, entertaining a wide circle of friends, including the Adamses, Websters and Calhouns. Under his guidance the *Intelligencer* supported in turn the Republican, Whig and Constitutional Democratic parties, endorsing Clay's Pan-American policy but observing with grim forebodings the election of Jackson. For a brief period he resided at Decatur House.

He was succeeded there by the King brothers, the "accomplished gentlemen" described by Mr. Tayloe. Sons of Rufus King, they had been educated in England while their father was American Minister to the Court of St. James. The elder was John Alsop King, who served as Secretary of Legation in London for his father, and afterwards became Governor of New York. The younger brother, James Gore King, preferred the financial world to politics, and became president of the New York and Erie Railroad. He has been described as "a leading spirit in the select social circles that foregathered on Manhattan Island in the early Nineteenth century." As a political interlude he chose a term in Congress, as Representative from New Jersey. The two brothers were in Congress at the same time, and the Congressional Directory for 1850 ingeniously listed their residence as "Private, corner 16½ and H Streets." For both of them a term in Washington politics was only an incident in their careers.

After the departure of the King brothers, Decatur House was occupied for a short time by William Appleton, a Boston merchant, who served several terms in Congress. According to Mr. Tayloe, "He was particularly a benevolent man, so much so that on a complaint by his steward, during a very cold spell of weather, that his wood, which had been left on the sidewalk, was fast diminishing, he replied, 'I think it had better not be put away while the weather remains so cold.' "

CHAPTER IX

STATESMEN OF THE LOST CAUSE

WASHINGTON on the eve of the Civil War was tense and turbulent. The political scene reflected the approaching "irrepressible conflict," and passions ran high as men drew apart into two hostile camps. As early as 1857 there was rioting in the city's streets, and two years later John Brown's raid brought consternation to the Capital, hemmed in as it was by Southern Maryland and Virginia. In the Senate it was facetiously suggested that Washington was in danger of becoming the capital of the Confederacy.

There was much sympathy in the city toward the Southern cause. At the aristocratic St. John's Church the parishioners were largely Southerners, and the rector offered public prayers for the success of the Confederacy. In a particularly difficult position were the Southerners serving in Congress at this time. Nominally a functioning part of the Federal Government, they were becoming increasingly convinced that the Union could not be preserved, and saw no practical course but the creation of another nation. Soon many of them would be statesmen under another flag, but meanwhile they were in the camp of the enemy, so to speak. Their position was perilous; their time was short; their faces were grave. From 1857 on, Decatur House became the residence of men of the Confederacy.

The first of these was Howell Cobb of Georgia, who occupied Decatur House while Secretary of the Treasury in the administration of President Buchanan. A former governor of Georgia, his whole political career had been overshadowed by one issue, that of secession. At first Cobb took such a moderate stand that his enemies accused him of straddling the issue. But when the show-down came Howell Cobb took the only course open to a Georgia gentleman. He joined the Southern cause, and in 1861 became chairman of the Secession Convention that met in Montgomery, Alabama, to create the Confederate States of America.

Throughout his life Howell Cobb had typified the best traditions of the South. A member of the plantation aristocracy of Georgia, he represented one of the leading families of the state, distinguished for prestige and wealth. Along with this went a record of public service; his grandfather had been a delegate to the Constitutional Convention of 1795, while his father and several uncles and cousins had held various legislative and Congressional positions. With such a background, Cobb was born September 7, 1815, at his father's home in Jefferson County, in the cotton country of middle Georgia.

His early life followed the usual plantation pattern, after which he took up the study of law and was admitted to the bar in 1836. At nineteen he married Mary Ann Lamar, of another old Georgia family. His career in public affairs began at an early age, for at twenty-two he was appointed a solicitor-general for the state, and he was elected to Congress in 1842, when not yet twenty-seven years old.

In Congress he was involved immediately in the major issues of the time, including the extension of slavery to the Western territories. He supported the annexation of Texas and President Polk's declaration of war on Mexico. But he opposed Calhoun's projected political bloc of Southern states, believing that a united country was more to the South's advantage. "After one of the most spectacular fights ever seen in Congress," says a recent authority, "Cobb was elected Speaker of the House in December 1849 on the sixty-third ballot."

The one issue, however, that overshadowed everything else was the right of secession. Cobb stood "for the Union and compromise." When he was nominated in 1851 for the governorship of Georgia there was a bitter campaign in which he opposed secessionism. Though attacked and heckled for evading the issue, Cobb was elected by the greatest majority known up to then. It was a triumph for his policy of moderation.

The tide of events, however, was against moderation, and Cobb was defeated in the next campaign for the governship. He returned to Congress, and subsequently his friend President Buchanan appointed him Secretary of the Treasury. It was the last and the highest office he would hold in the Federal Government.

JUDAH P. BENJAMIN, SENATOR FROM LOUISIANA

During this period from 1857 to 1860, while he resided in Decatur House, there was a grim decision to be made—the transfer of his allegiance from the country that he and his ancestors had served. Under the circumstances the entertainments at Decatur House were scarcely gay and lighthearted; gone were the days when a frivolous woman could be important. Long and serious the discussions must have been; at some point the die had to be cast. In 1860 Lincoln was elected; Howell Cobb declared for secession.

From this point on the sands were running fast. The following year a Secession Convention met at Montgomery and organized the government of the Confederacy. Cobb presided over the convention, and some favored him in place of Jefferson Davis to head the Southern cause. Instead, he organized the 16th Georgia regiment and led it on the battlefield, being promoted to Major General. At the end of the war he resumed law practice, but died suddenly in 1868.

Even in the midst of gathering war clouds Decatur House had its lighter moments, providing a romantic interlude in the life of Judah P. Benjamin. Of all the statesmen of the Confederacy, Benjamin was one of the most colorful. A Louisiana lawyer, of Portuguese Jewish ancestry, he became ultimately a statesman of the Confederacy. Among his chief concerns was his wife Natalie.

Benjamin was born in 1811 in the British West Indies, on the island of St. Thomas. As a boy he moved with his family to Charleston, South Carolina, where he attended Fayetteville Academy. In 1826 he went to Yale for two years, but left to enter business in New Orleans. He gave English lessons among French families, and married a pupil, Natalie St. Martin, in 1833.

After studying law in a notary's office, he was admitted to the bar and quickly attained prominence in a celebrated case concerning the international aspects of the brig *Creole,* involving the status of slavery under American and international law. As a successful lawyer he rapidly acquired wealth, and became a sugar planter. But the failure of a friend involved him in financial liabilities; he lost his plantation and returned to law.

His home life was far from unruffled. His wife Natalie was a woman of little education; Mrs. Jefferson Davis later commented on her "unassisted human nature." This she combined with an extravagance that must have vexed the soul of her prudent husband. "Oh, talk not to me of economy!" she wrote him on one occasion, "It is so fatiguing." One can imagine his lacerated feelings.

After a few years of married life Natalie, a devout Catholic, left him and went to Paris to live. Benjamin continued to reside with her parents, and cherished the hope of an eventual reconciliation.

A natural conservative, he joined the Whig party and was elected to the state legislature. Some years of political activity followed, and then in 1852 he went to Washington as a Senator from Louisiana. In the Senate he ably identified himself with the promotion of commerce, and helped organize the Illinois Central Railroad. Commerce for the South was his particular hobby. Like many others he believed that the South, by the development of commerce, could restore the sectional balance of power against the North, which had been upset in the Compromise of 1850.

An ardent Southerner, Benjamin believed the South needed a party of its own, and transferred his allegiance from the Whigs to the Democrats. Re-elected to the Senate in 1856, he became a leader of the secession bloc in Congress, going so far as to urge that Louisiana act independently to separate herself from the Union. Thus he and Cobb typified the two poles of Southern thought, the extremists and moderates, in the years before the war.

It was in 1859, at the height of the sectional crisis, that Benjamin decided upon the reconquest of his alienated wife. In that year he leased Decatur House and filled it with ostentatious and costly furnishings, "the envy of local connoisseurs." All this was bait for Natalie to return to the fold, as mistress of this enviable establishment. The lure was effective.

There was, however, one chilling possibility that caused him much concern, namely, how Washington society would accept his long-absent wife. Naturally under the circumstances there was a considerable amount of gossip about his enforced bachelorhood, and the sudden appearance of a truant spouse was bound to create a minor sensation. There was certainly ground for doubt whether Mrs. Benjamin would be received, particularly since Decatur House recalled to mind only too vividly the fate of Peggy Eaton. But this was a chance he had to take. Meanwhile the same year La Fayette

Square was electrified by a sensational homicide, in which the city's District Attorney, Philip Barton Key, was fatally shot by General Daniel E. Sickles in the role of an aggrieved husband.

Natalie, then about forty-five, arrived from Paris and took her place as the wife of Senator Benjamin and the mistress of Decatur House. Immediately a social problem was created. The leaders of Washington society foregathered at the home of Mrs. Clement Clay to consider the situation. There were "rumored delinquencies" concerning the lady, but as the wife of a ranking Senator she deserved visiting courtesies. The ladies were of two minds, and were unable to reach an agreement, so they decided to present the problem to their husbands.

When Mrs. Clay put the matter to her husband, the Senator from Alabama, he replied, "By all means, call. You have nothing to do with the lady's private life, and, as a mark of esteem to a statesman of her husband's prominence, it will be better to call." Mrs. Clay and other ladies accepted this.

The event at Decatur House was described by Mrs. Clay: "Upon a certain day, therefore, it was agreed that we should pay a 'mass' call, going in a body. We drove accordingly, in dignity and in state, and, truth to tell, in soberness and ceremony, to the mansion aforenamed. It was the lady's reception day. We entered the drawing-room with great circumspection, tempering our usually cordial manner with a fine prudence; we paid our devoirs to the hostess and retired."

To the curious, Mrs. Benjamin proved beautiful and "very, very gay." Her husband evidently worshipped her, and seemed intent on fulfilling her every wish. Under the gaiety, however, there were signs of unhappiness. Some fancied she resented being married to Benjamin. Perhaps it was merely that she preferred life in Paris.

There followed a period of curious suspense. Mrs. Benjamin did not return the calls. Time passed and social gossip was active. Mrs. Clay continues: "Now a curious retribution overtook us, social faint-hearts that we were; for, though we heard much gossip of the regality and originality of one or more dinners given to several of the diplomatic corps (the lady especially affected the French Legation), I never heard of a gathering of Washingtonians at her home, nor of invitations extended to them, nor, indeed, anything more of her until two months had flown."

Behind Mrs. Benjamin's curious unresponsiveness to Washington social overtures was a matter of domestic rift. Suddenly it broke into the open.

"Arab-like, the lady rose in the night, 'silently folded her tent and stole away' (to meet a handsome German officer, it was said), leaving our calls unanswered, save by the sending of her card, and her silver and china and crystal, her paintings, and hangings, and furniture to be auctioned off to the highest bidder!"

Natalie returned to Paris, with her daughter Ninette, then about eighteen. Her husband sought no divorce.

Benjamin made his farewell speech in the Senate on February 4, 1861, and withdrew quietly. For him it was the end of many things. Leaving Decatur House for the last time, he looked about sadly, saying that he had known the deepest sorrow in the house he had prepared for his deepest happiness.

He went South at once, and joined the provisional government of Jefferson Davis as Attorney General. Shortly afterwards he became Secretary for War, and then for three years was chief Secretary of State of the Confederacy. When the bitter struggle was over he remained loyal to Jefferson Davis to the end, escaping with him after Appomattox. Eluding capture, he made his way to the Florida coast, and got away in an open boat. Finally he reached England, and began life anew as an English barrister, achieving such success as to be known as "the American Disraeli."

Judah P. Benjamin was the last occupant of Decatur House prior to the Civil War. During the war years La Fayette Square was the scene of much military activity. The Federal government took over Decatur House, the Dolly Madison house, the Blair house, and others, using them as military headquarters or emergency offices. Soldiers guarding the White House camped in the Square, trampled its flower beds, and hung their washing from the Jackson monument.

The equestrian statute of Andrew Jackson had been erected in the center of the Square in 1853. It was the work of a young sculptor from Georgia, named Clark Mills, who was something of a pioneer in his field. He operated under certain handicaps; he

Harris & Ewing

STATUE OF ANDREW JACKSON IN LaFAYETTE PARK, WASHINGTON, ERECTED IN 1853, AND BELIEVED TO BE THE OLDEST STATUE IN THE DISTRICT OF COLUMBIA

had never seen an equestrian statue, nor had he ever seen General Jackson. He set up his own forge, and melted down some cannon that Jackson had captured in the War of 1812. From books and hearsay he produced his design of the general on horseback, and succeeded in casting it successfully. The romantic, carousel-like figure was unveiled with great ceremony; it was indeed a unique accomplishment, quickly forgotten in the onset of the war years.

CHAPTER X

THE PATH OF EMPIRE

I

THE CANNONS BOOMED as General Grant's train arrived in Washington, and great crowds turned out to welcome the former President, returning in 1878 after a tour of the world. The General and Mrs. Grant were driven up Pennsylvania Avenue, which was draped with flags and bunting and lined with crowds of cheering people. A man shouted "I was with him at Shiloh!" The procession made its way to La Fayette Square, and halted at Decatur House.

On his visits to Washington General Grant habitually stayed at Decatur House, the home of his old friend, General Edward Fitzgerald Beale. To welcome him on this occasion a reception was held that evening in his honor. "The beautiful drawing rooms on the second floor were the scene of a brilliant company," declared a contemporary account. "General Beale greeted the guests at the doorway at the head of the stairs, Mrs. and Miss Beale standing just within the gold embroidered portieres of the main drawing room. General and Mrs. Grant stood at the other side of the room, and were the center of a large group during the arrival of the guests. Mrs. Beale wore on this occasion a trained toilet of black satin, with point lace and jet trimmings, and diamond ornaments, including a jeweled tiara in the hair. Mrs. Grant was attired in a black velvet reception dress, with corsage finished at neck and sleeves with point lace; her ornaments were of large diamonds, around them a band of tiny horseshoes, set with diamonds, across the high coiffure. A handsome supper was served in the dining room during the evening, and the library was used as a tea room."

The following day, after attending St. John's Church, General Grant and General Beale drove out to the latter's country place to inspect the Arabian horses presented to Grant by the Sultan of Turkey. These two stallions, "Linden Tree" and "Leopard," were rare specimens from the Sultan's private stables, and their arrival in Washington had excited much comment. After this brief excursion the two gentlemen returned to the city, where a round of entertainments and receptions awaited them. One of these events was a state dinner at the White House, where they ate from "that grotesque set of china" then in official use, "upon which stalk and flounder the various game birds, animals and fishes of this continent." After a week's entertainment, General Grant and his wife departed for Florida.

II

All during the nineteenth century the forces of American history pressed westward. Of the men of that period, none were more energetic and colorful than those who helped to subdue the vast territory stretching out to the Pacific. In an era of commanding personalities, Edward Fitzgerald Beale was a unique and outstanding figure, whose dynamic life was devoted mainly to this great historical movement, the winning of the West. Bayard Taylor summarized his career as "A pioneer in the path of empire."

His own roots lay deep in American history, as evidenced by his lineage. In later life he wrote: "Of my ancestors in America, one fell while in the act of speaking to Colonel Washington on the field of Braddock's defeat; another fell at the side of John Paul Jones. My grandfather received a gold medal from Congress for his capture, in the *Constellation,* of two French frigates, both his superiors in guns and men. My father received a medal from his country by order of Congress, for distinguished gallantry in the battle of Lake Champlain." To this list it might be added that he himself continued to exemplify this great tradition.

Edward Fitzgerald Beale was born February 4, 1822, at his father's estate "Bloomingdale" in the District of Columbia, a mile or so north of the Capitol. The Beales were direct descendants of Colonel the Honorable Thomas Beale, a prominent figure of early colonial days. He was appointed by Charles II as Councilman of Virginia, and came to the colony prior to 1649, becoming a landowner in York County and a vestryman of Bruton Church. One of his descendants was George Beale of Bloomingdale, a naval officer who served with distinction in the War of 1812. Preserved

THE ARABIAN STALLIONS "LINDEN TREE" (TOP) AND "LEOPARD" (BOTTOM),
PRESENTED TO EX-PRESIDENT GENERAL U. S. GRANT BY THE SULTAN OF TURKEY.
FROM PAINTINGS IN DECATUR HOUSE

PRESIDENT U. S. GRANT AND PRINCE LI HUNG CHÁNG, MINISTER OF FOREIGN AFFAIRS
OF CHINA. FROM A PHOTOGRAPH IN DECATUR HOUSE

COMMODORE THOMAS TRUXTUN, GRANDFATHER OF EDWARD F. BEALE.
FROM AN ORIGINAL PAINTING BY BASS OTIS
(Property of Long Island Historical Society, Long Island, N. Y.)

CHASED SILVER CUP PRESENTED TO CAPTAIN THOMAS TRUXTUN, U.S.N.,
BY LLOYDS COFFEE HOUSE TO COMMEMORATE HIS VICTORY
OVER THE FRENCH FRIGATE "INSURGENTE" IN 1799

in the family archives is a letter to him from the Secretary of the Navy:

NAVY DEPARTMENT, February 10, 1820.

Sir: In compliance with a resolution of Congress I am directed by the President to present to you a silver medal as a testimony of the high sense entertained by Congress of the gallantry and good conduct and services in the decisive and splendid victory gained on Lake Champlain on the 11th of September, 1814, over a British squadron of superior force.

Yours, most respectfully,

SMITH THOMPSON
Secretary of the Navy

To GEORGE BEALE, ESQ.
Purser, U. S. Navy

The wife of George Beale, Emily, was the youngest daughter of Commodore Thomas Truxtun, one of the original founders of the American naval tradition, first as a privateer captain during the Revolution and subsequently as one of the heroes of the original naval force of the nation. The Commodore's daughter was so notable for her personal beauty that she and her sisters were known as "the beautiful Truxtuns," whom Aaron Burr declared were the handsomest women of that period. From both sides of his family the young boy, Edward Fitzgerald Beale, inherited a naval tradition, and it was a foregone conclusion that he should enter the naval service.

During his boyhood in Washington an episode occurred in which he virtually "fought his way into the Navy." Even as a child he took an active interest in the fervid politics of the period, as an admirer of Andrew Jackson. One day, among a group of other boys, he was engaged in forcible expression of his political views, under an arch at the southern entrance to the White House. While the boys were fighting a tall gentleman appeared. Seizing them by the collar, he asked what the boys were fighting about. The reply was brief and spirited. "Ned" Beale declared he was fighting for Jackson.

"I am Jackson," declared the gentleman. To the astonished boys he added, "I never forget the men or boys who are willing to fight for me, but I don't wish them to do it all the time. Now put on your coats."

The promise bore fruit in subsequent years. When "Ned" Beale was fourteen, and a student at Georgetown College, he prevailed upon his mother to seek a naval appointment for him. Mrs. Beale and her son presented themselves at the White House for a call on President Jackson. The old general listened attentively while Mrs. Beale requested that her son be given a warrant as a midshipman. She recounted the naval careers of his father and grandfather, but the President seemed to hesitate. At this point the boy spoke up: "Mother, let me speak to General Jackson in my own behalf."

Then he recalled to the President the episode of the boyish battle on the White House lawn. At once the President picked up his pen and wrote the Secretary of the Navy, "Give this boy an immediate warrant." In a few hours "Ned" Beale was on the Navy list.

His training began on the receiving ship *Independence* at Philadelphia, then used as a naval training school. After completing his course he was assigned in October, 1845, to the frigate *Congress*, under the command of Commodore Stockton. They set sail for California, where "Ned" Beale was to play an historic role in that new territory.

The young midshipman was catapulted into prominence immediately by circumstances of the voyage. Historians believe that in the West Indies Commodore Stockton obtained important news concerning the disposition of British naval forces in regard to California. The actual story of what happened was a matter of considerable speculation at the time, nor has the passage of years clarified the situation. All we know is that Commodore Stockton selected Beale as a courier of important dispatches, and transferred him to another ship going in the opposite direction. Beale reached his destination in a roundabout way, for the vessel carried him to England, where he took passage on another ship to America, arriving finally in Washington in March, 1846. Here he received a promotion to the rank of Master, and sailed for Panama, overtaking Commodore Stockton in the *Congress* at Callao, Peru. Of the nature of his secret mission nothing is known. In later

Edward Fitzgerald Beale,
Lieutenant, U. S. Navy

years Beale said: "Commodore Stockton never removed the seal
of secrecy from my lips."

War with Mexico had broken out that same year, and hostilities
had already begun when the *Congress* arrived at Monterey,
California, July 20th. They found that California had just been
annexed to the United States.

III

California was named from Ordoñez de Montalvo's romance
of chivalry, *Las Sergas de Esplandian,* which described it as an
island "to the right of the Indies." Various explorers came to this
vaguely defined area, which for two centuries continued to be
known as an island. The development of Califorña began with the
introduction of the Spanish mission system, and for a long period
it remained an integral part of Mexico. In the early nineteenth
century there was a series of *opéra bouffe* wars and revolutions,
accompanied by a wave of republicanism. The first link with the
United States was by way of trade, which had a decisive influence.
In 1835 President Jackson's offer to purchase the territory was
declined, but soon after that American settlers began reaching
California overland.

The territory was a rich prize that stimulated foreign intrigue.
The Russians had a post at Bodega Bay, and at one time it appeared
that the British might take over California. To forestall such a
move an American naval commander, Commodore Thomas ap
Catesby Jones, raised his country's flag at Monterey in 1842.
Finding his information unsubstantiated, he lowered the flag with
apologies the following day. But the act was symbolical of
California's future.

The Mexican War, which broke out in May, 1846, clinched the
issue finally. While General Zachary Taylor was fighting the
Mexicans in Texas, and General Winfield Scott proceeded southward
to capture Mexico City, naval forces were sent around the Horn
to secure control of the Pacific Coast. An "Army of the West"
was assembled at Fort Leavenworth to invade New Mexico and
push on to the Pacific, to effect a junction with the fleet. This little
army under General Stephen Kearny, marched 900 miles to
Santa Fé, at which point it was learned that the operation was

fruitless. The American Navy had already taken over California. On July 7, 1846, Commodore John D. Sloat had raised the American flag at Monterey, and California was proclaimed a part of the United States. Two weeks later, Commodore Stockton arrived with reinforcements, and assumed command.

The Navy was now faced with the problem of rescuing General Kearny, who had gotten himself surrounded by a Mexican army near San Pasquale. Receiving an appeal for help, Commodore Stockton dispatched a naval detachment to San Pasquale. One of the officers of this detachment was Lieutenant Beale. After a forced march they joined Kearny and found him in a precarious situation, his army exhausted by the long journey and outnumbered by the surrounding Mexicans. The expected attack came at San Pasquale on December 6th. The naval force fought shoulder to shoulder with Kearny's men, and among those who distinguished themselves in the battle was Lieutenant Beale. The outcome of the battle was dubious for a long period, and Kearny himself was wounded. But in the end the Americans held the field, though greatly reduced in numbers. In proportion to the forces, the casualty rate exceeded any other battle of the Mexican War.

After the battle, however, Kearny's forces were still in desperate straits. He withdrew to a position in the nearby hills, but could not shake off the pursuing Mexicans. In this new position he was temporarily safe, but he could not move and his communications were cut off. The Mexican commander was content to wait; he knew the American forces were effectively bottled up in the hills, and in time could be starved out. He had no intention of storming their position by a frontal assault, with many casualties. As time passed, his surrounding forces were strengthened, while the Americans became weaker.

The situation of the Americans looked bad. Kearny's men had been on short rations for days; they were hungry and exhausted. Their scanty food supplies were eked out by the slaughter of their mules, and they had named their position "Mule Hill." But there was little water available, and the mules were almost gone. Without relief the little detachment was doomed. The Mexican forces, camped about the hill in a large circle, could have rushed the position and overpowered the exhausted defenders. Instead, they waited for starvation to decide the issue.

The only hope now was to get a courier through the lines for aid. The nearest available help was at San Diego, some forty or fifty miles away. If a courier succeeded in breaking through the surrounding besiegers, he would still have a difficult journey through hostile country. "If messengers went at all they would have to go on foot, and to undertake the journey would seem like embarking on an expedition of forlorn hope, as all Mexicans, whether soldier or civilian, under the state of things that existed would consider they would be rendering both God and their country good service by shooting any American that came in sight."

At this point Lieutenant Beale volunteered to make the desperate effort to get word to Commodore Stockton at San Diego. Kearny decided to let him undertake the mission. The likelihood of success would be multiplied by sending three couriers instead of one. The second volunteer was the famous scout, Kit Carson, and the third was Beale's Delaware Indian servant. The trio waited for darkness to make their way through the enemy lines. After brief but fervent farewells they started out.

Lieutenant Beale had a fair knowledge of the country, having covered the same route a few weeks before in the first reconnaissance expedition. They evaded the enemy pickets and made their way that night through the hilly countryside. At daybreak the journey became more hazardous, as they had to avoid all people along the way, and keep a sharp watch for enemy scouts. Spurred on by the knowledge of the desperate position of his comrades, Beale pushed ahead steadily without rest, but the rugged countryside made travel difficult, and it was not until nightfall that he dragged himself wearily into San Diego, suffering from exhaustion. Kit Carson arrived a day later.

Reaching the headquarters of Commodore Stockton, Lieutenant Beale reported the dire position of the American forces. Immediately the "Assembly" was sounded, and a relief expedition of several hundred men was sent at once to the aid of General Kearny. They arrived just in time, for the starved and exhausted defenders could not have held out much longer. Their rations had been gone two days; the Mexicans might have carried the position by assault, but fortunately their commander had elected to starve them out, and his strategy failed. With the arrival of reinforcements General Kearny's troops were safe, thanks to Lieutenant Beale.

For his heroic feat, Beale received from his fellow officers a presentation gold sword and epaulets with this inscription:

"Presented by the officers of the United States Navy on the station at San Diego, California, to Lieutenant Edward F. Beale, of the United States Navy, for his gallant conduct in the charge upon the Mexican forces at San Pasquale and San Bernardino, and his carrying intelligence to San Diego of the position of General Kearny through the enemy's lines at great personal risk on the 6th and 7th of December, 1846."

The hazardous trip proved nearly fatal to Beale, who was hospitalized for days afterwards. Upon his recovery he was summoned by Commodore Stockton. In recognition of his feat, Beale was selected to carry the dispatches to Washington reporting the events in California. The Commodore's instructions read as follows:

"I have selected you to be the bearer of the accompanying dispatches to the Navy Department in consequence of your heroic conduct in volunteering to leave General Kearny's camp (then surrounded by the enemy) to go to the garrison of San Diego for assistance, and because of the perils and hardships you underwent during that dangerous journey to procure aid for your suffering fellow-soldiers."

On this trip across the continent Beale was accompanied by twelve soldiers and the famous Indian scout, Kit Carson. A bond of friendship quickly developed between the young naval officer and the frontiersman. Carson's name was a byword throughout the West. He had been born in Kentucky in 1809, but his family moved to Missouri, where the boy grew up, and at the age of seventeen joined a wagon train bound West. From then on he had many adventures as a scout and guide, until the name Kit Carson became a synonym for frontier skill and daring.

In February, 1847, Beale and Carson set out for Washington, bearing the great news of the conquest of California. Beale was still weak from his recent ordeal, and Carson had to lift him on and off his horse, not thinking at first that he would survive. But with Carson's generous care Beale recovered his strength for the

Gold sword and epaulettes presented to Lieut. Edward F. Beale, U.S.N., by his fellow officers for his services at San Pasquale

AUTOGRAPHED PHOTOGRAPH OF KIT CARSON, THE FAMOUS SCOUT
IN DECATUR HOUSE

fatiguing and dangerous journey, much of it through hostile Indian territory. They followed a southerly route until they reached the Gila River, a tributary of the Colorado, where their main encounter with the Indians occurred. Carson discovered that the party was being followed stealthily throughout the day, and anticipated an attack that night. An old frontier ruse was decided upon. Making an early encampment, the party built fires and ostentatiously settled for the night. After darkness fell, they silently broke camp and moved on to another site. The attack developed as expected, but the changed camp site deceived the Indians, and the concerted onslaught was fruitless. The Indians scattered, and by the time they located the quarry they could muster only a small attacking force, which was repulsed.

Kit Carson has left the following account of Beale that night: "Things whirring like birds on the flight wuz flying over us, as I wuz trying to sleep by the campfire, and Ned wuz sleepin' or leastwise he wuz snorin'. Then suddenly he sits up an' says, 'What's that, Don Kit?' and I says, 'Them's arrers' and they wuz. And, could you believe it, before I could hold him down, Ned was wrapping his buffalo robe about him and standing in the fire kicking out the embers. 'Now,' sez he, as them arrers came whizzin' along like a raft of geese going south before er north wind, 'Now,' sez he, 'Don Kit, they won't be able to get our directions any more, and you know they don't dare rush us.' Then he tumbled down on the ground and went on with his sleepin'."

During the remainder of the journey the party had repeated brushes with the Indians, but crossed the plains successfully to St. Louis, where they attracted enormous public interest. Proceeding onward, they reached Washington in May, 1847, with the welcome news that California had joined the Union. Beale and Carson were greeted with much acclaim, and curious crowds followed them in the streets, pressing forward to shake their hands. Carson stayed at Beale's home "Bloomingdale," but insisted on sleeping outdoors, if only on the veranda. He preferred to meet visitors out in the open, saying "I allays see folks out in the road."

Their stay in Washington was short, for they were ordered to return immediately with dispatches for the West Coast. The return journey ended in a near disaster, for Beale was wounded in an

Indian skirmish on the plains. Carson guarded and nursed him, and managed to get him back to St. Louis. Beale then returned to his home in the East, to recuperate and await further orders. Anxious to get back West, he asked an old friend of the family, Senator Thomas H. Benton, of Missouri, to intercede with the Navy Department for appointment on another mission. This was granted, and in October he received orders to return to the Pacific coast with naval dispatches. He took ship via Panama to Callao, and sailed north to Mazatlan. Here he served on shore in command of a naval detachment. News of the peace with Mexico arrived the following year.

IV

When a man named Marshall was working on the construction of a sawmill for Captain John Sutter, in the vicinity of Sacramento, he observed yellow flakes in the mill race. This discovery, on January 24, 1848, was kept secret a few weeks but the news leaked out. A newspaper editor ran through the streets of San Francisco waving a bottle of gold dust and shouting, "Gold! Gold! Gold!" On March 15 the San Francisco Californian announced: "GOLD MINE FOUND." The Army and Navy authorities promptly investigated the rumors and penned their dispatches.

At this time Beale was an acting lieutenant aboard the *Ohio*, flagship of Commodore Thomas ap Catesby Jones, commander of the Pacific Squadron. He had been temporarily detached for unwelcome shore duty because he had incurred the Commodore's displeasure. An able caricaturist, Beale had depicted the old sea dog as a windy storyteller, recounting ancient memories. Word of the caricature got back to Jones, and the young lieutenant was sent ashore. Beale's biographer writes: "Some of the officers saw in Beale's subsequent selection to carry dispatches and the news of gold across Mexico a further evidence of the Commodore's hostility." In any case, the Commodore summoned Beale in July, 1848, and said to him, "I'm ordering you to Washington with dispatches. How soon can you leave?" Beale replied, "At once, sir."

"Good," said the Commodore. "Colonel Mason of the Army is planning to send a courier also. Never let it be said that the Army

EDWARD FITZGERALD BEALE, LIEUT., U.S.N.,
DRESSED IN MEXICAN DISGUISE FOR HIS RIDE ACROSS MEXICO IN 1849
BEARING NAVAL DISPATCHES AND THE FIRST SAMPLES OF
GOLD FROM CALIFORNIA TO REACH WASHINGTON
FROM AN OIL PAINTING IN DECATUR HOUSE

beat the Navy in anything. I've picked you for this job because you're as much at home on the trail as the teakwood deck. In fact, I sometimes think you're a blasted landlubber at heart. What about some gold to take back with you?"

"I already have some dust and nuggets of my own that I traded for quinine," Beale answered.

"Excellent. You will shove off as soon as the flag secretary has completed my dispatches to the Secretary of the Navy. And remember this: Get to Washington, D. C., before that Army courier!"

The acting governor of California, Colonel Richard Mason, had chosen the other courier, Lieutenant Lucian Loesser, of the Third Engineer Corps. Loesser carried a tea caddy containing gold samples and dust, estimated to be worth $3,000. Inter-service rivalry quickly transformed the mission into a race between the two couriers.

Beale boldly chose the quickest but most arduous route, overland through Mexico, while his Army rival sailed comfortably to Panama, to cross the Isthmus and take another ship. Beale departed two weeks earlier, on August 1, 1848. Crossing the Gulf of California from La Paz to the naval base, he hired a small vessel to carry him down the coast to San Blas, where the land journey would begin.

At San Blas the Mexican governor said to him: "Señor, an American like yourself could not travel a dozen miles in Mexico without being robbed and murdered."

When Beale expressed surprise, the governor explained: "The troops of Mariano Paredes have deserted and turned bandit. These *ladrones* are desperate, señor, and would not hesitate to kill you for the horse you ride."

Nevertheless, Beale prepared for his thousand-mile journey overland, via Guadalajara, Mexico City and Vera Cruz. This was the most colorful trip of his career. Outfitted in frontier clothes, and speaking fluent Spanish, he could make his way through the country with a minimum of attention. With his browned skin he could pass as a Mexican, and the four six-barrelled revolvers that he carried were his best passport, along with his Bowie knife.

On the 12th of August he left San Blas and rode overland day and night, spurred by the urgency of the occasion. He and his

Mexican guide fought off three bandits near Tepic, but the episode persuaded him to take other precautions. Against the eventuality of his death, he copied his dispatches, and arranged at a town en route for them to follow him by mail to Mexico City. Before reaching Guadalajara he eluded a band of pursuers armed with carbines. At another point he found the dead bodies of eleven travelers who had been murdered shortly before. Another hazard was the onset of the rainy season, when incessant storms made travel more difficult.

After a 725-mile trip in eight days since leaving San Blas, he reached Mexico City, covered with the mud of travel. There the American Minister, Nathan Clifford, insisted that he rest for a few days and carry additional dispatches. Here in Mexico City Beale met an American officer in the Casino on the Plaza, Ulysses S. Grant, afterwards his close friend. From Mexico City Beale hastened on to Vera Cruz, retracing the route followed by Cortez, and covering the 275 miles in forty-eight hours. There his Mexican guide broke down, his mind impaired. Beale set sail from Vera Cruz in the sloop-of-war *Germantown,* and reached Mobile, Alabama. There he boarded the stagecoach and arrived in Washington in the record-breaking time of forty-seven days.

In an article entitled "He Won the Gold Dust Derby" a recent writer declares, "The forgotten man of American history, Lieutenant Beale, won a gruelling cross-continent race . . . to deliver to the Atlantic seaboard the most electrifying news of the last century—the discovery of gold in California." The 4,000-mile journey ended September 16, 1848, when Beale reached Washington with his saddlebags stuffed with dispatches for the Secretary of State and the Secretary of the Navy. Of greater public interest, however, was the small bottle of gold dust that he carried— substantial evidence of the great discovery. Beale was asked to appear before the United States Senate to give a personal account of his expedition. He was introduced by an old friend, Senator Benton of Missouri, and Senator Foote of Mississippi. After describing the gold discovery and the bringing of the news across Mexico, Beale went on to discuss the significance of the discovery for the future of the West.

"There is danger," he said, "that California may starve because even the farmers have gone crazy with the gold fever." He described the depopulation of towns as their inhabitants rushed to the gold fields; even soldiers and sailors were deserting in droves to seek their fortune. The gold rush was on.

Those who were incredulous over the discovery were silenced by President Polk's official recognition of it in his message to Congress that same year. In the meantime Beale's sample nuggets and dust were the center of avid curiosity; people followed him in the streets in hopes of getting a glimpse of the gold. He politely declined the following offer from Mr. Barnum, the circus proprietor:

BARNUM'S MUSEUM, Philadelphia
May 29, 1849

Lieutenant Beale:

Mr. Harding of the *Inquirer* has just informed me that you have in your possession an 8 lb. lump of California gold. As I am always anxious to procure novelties for public gratification, I write this to say that I should be glad to purchase the lump at its valuation if you will dispose of it, and if not, that I should like to procure it for exhibition for a few weeks. A line in reply will much oblige.

Your obt. servt.

P. T. BARNUM

Actually the disposition of the gold was simple and logical. Half of it he donated to the U.S. Patent Office in Washington. The remainder of it was made into a wedding ring, for his marriage to his childhood sweetheart and fiancée, Mary E. Edwards.

Before his marriage, however, there was another overland trip to be made to California. In October of the same year the Navy's premier dispatch carrier left for Fort Leavenworth on the Missouri, and a month later pushed onward from there with a command of seventeen men, "raw recruits and a few adventurers." The coming of winter made the journey unduly severe, and the party suffered greatly, but with indomitable effort they reached Santa Fé on Christmas Day, "on foot and nearly naked," as he afterwards reported. Pressing on, the party encountered even more rigorous conditions, and nearly half of the men deserted, probably to their death. The remainder reached San Francisco in April, having proven the feasibility of a midwinter crossing of the continent. After only three days in San Francisco, Beale started back to Washington, arriving there June 17, 1849.

V

Ten days after his arrival, on June 27, 1849, Lieutenant Beale married Mary E. Edwards, daughter of Representative Samuel Edwards, of Chester, Pennsylvania. The Edwards were an old Quaker family, whose ancestors had come over with William Penn in 1682. Samuel Edwards was a pivotal figure in Congress for many years, and afterwards Collector of Customs at Chester, Pennsylvania, where the marriage took place. Immediately the young couple left for Washington, where Beale received his orders for California. He started at once, and returned in December from a round trip across the continent.

By now Beale's exploits had made him a nationally-known figure, for many accounts of his adventures had been published in American newspapers and magazines. These accounts were often concerned, of course, with the more picturesque episodes of his travels. One of these may be summarized in part, to show how he appeared in the eyes of his contemporaries. It was published in the *North American* of June 12, 1849, and described "the last journey to California from which he has lately returned."

One evening in the Gila country Beale established camp, and went out hunting for food supplies for the party. Six miles from camp he killed a deer, and was dressing the carcass when a group of mounted Apaches swept over the hillside. Knowing that a solitary white man faced certain death at their hands, he mounted his horse and rode for his life, the Apaches in hot pursuit. Halfway to camp he was horrified to see one of his own men, who had strayed away from the others. At the sight of the Indians the man cried to Beale, "Save me! I am a husband and the father of six helpless children!" Without hesitation the lieutenant stopped, turned his horse over to the man, and told him, "Ride back to camp, and send them out to give my body decent burial." The man mounted and galloped off, leaving Beale to face the Apaches alone. He drew his revolver and sat down for better aim. In a moment or two the Indians arrived, but the horse and rider were a more attractive quarry than a man by himself, and they continued after the horseman. Beale circled carefully through the area and reached camp safely. The other man had escaped also, though wounded.

Such accounts of his exploits reached a wide audience, and made Beale more famous than he realized. At this time the great Arctic explorer, Sir John Franklin, was lost in the far north, and Beale was invited to join a rescue expedition that perhaps might reach the North Pole:

Dear Sir:—*

Although personally a stranger to you, the subject of this letter, will I trust, be its ample apology.

When I first volunteered to go in quest of Sir. Jno. Franklin and his companions, it was my purpose, if my application was successful, to have asked you to accompany me—for although you are recently married, I have not done your partner the injustice to class her among weak and frivolous wives, but rather, regarded her as one who would cheer you in an undertaking which would enhance your reputation and your name.

The long interval that was supinely suffered to elapse had nearly taken all hope, when a recent letter from the Rev'd Mr. Scoresby, written at the instance of Lady Franklin, has re-invigorated me. In that letter, I am told, that Lady F. and her friends place little reliance on the expedition now being equipped by the Admiralty, and which is to persue the route by Behring's straits. Their greatest hope is in us and the eastern route. If that lady carries her intention into effect and comes to this country, I have little doubt that an expedition will be authorized. I use the term authorized, because Congress may not feel justified in appropriating money, especially for such an object, while its sanction or that of the Executive would be necessary to a military organization, without which I presume, no officer of respectability would undertake it.

Should it be undertaken and I be appointed to lead it will you embark with me? Do not answer with precipitation, for I know that you will never withdraw a pledge, and I only wish to receive one after full deliberation.

---

* Original in the Beale archives.

If you decide to cast your lot with me, in the above event, I would of course stipulate that you should be second in command.

My reasons for applying to you are twofold—first physical, for my own constitution is weak, while yours, from all I can learn, is a vigorous and hardy one and secondly, you have the moral qualities, unshrinking courage and indomitable perseverance which are indispensable for such an undertaking.

It would be my aim to pass through Wellington Channel and make our winters quarters on the north shore of Melville Island. If in our route thither we were unsuccessful in one search, I would during the winter despatch parties to the north to reach the Pole if possible, the other to the west towards Behring's straits—the members of each party to be surmounted on skates, with light boats fixed on metallic sleigh runners. If neither of those parties should discover the English ships or their crews, there would be no longer doubt of their having perished. When the summer opened, therefore I would feel justified in making a bold push with the ship for Behring's Straits, through which if I could only succeed in carrying the Am. flags I could die content. Even at the worst, it is a noble cause to die in: But you have endearing attachments to the world, and I would not have you thoughtlessly link your fate with one so desolate as myself.

Please answer this at your leisure and let no editor of a paper see or hear anything of it.

Uncertain of your direction, I will send this to the department to be forwarded to you.

> With great respect,
> Your obt. Serv't.
> W. F. Lynch, U.S.N.
> Baltimore Jan'y, 11, 1850.

Lieut. E. F. Beale,
   U.S. Navy.

Beale undoubtedly felt that the rescue of Sir John Franklin was a laudable project, but should be left in the hands of those with previous knowledge and experience of the Arctic, and the suggestion was declined. It must have been an attractive offer, however, to one of his temperament and inclinations.

His marriage marked the beginning of a new period in his life. With a wife now, he was less attracted to adventurous expeditions through the West, and had to give more thought to the founding of a home and a family. At this point he received a business offer from his former commanding officer, Commodore Stockton, who had acquired extensive interests in California in conjunction with a great New York merchant, G. W. Aspinwall. They had become partners in a gold mining operation in California, which was on the verge of failure, and they hoped that Beale could retrieve or liquidate the situation. Upon receiving the offer, Beale decided to resign from the Navy and devote himself to business affairs, beginning with the following:

Philadelphia, Jan. 9th, 1851*

My dear Sir:

Upon reflection we have determined to consent to your going to California for the purpose of retrieving our affairs at the Gold Mines.

You will therefore proceed by the first steamer to California, and take upon yourself entire charge and superintendence of our Gold operations in that state, and all the property belonging thereto.

You are fully aware of the great expense which has been incurred by our mining operations, and the necessity we are under to have those expenses stopped. You will therefore see Mr. Norris as soon as possible after your arrival at San Francisco.

If upon consultation with him and Captains Rube and Hart you find that our expenses are as great, and the prospects of remuneration as bad as they seem to be by Mr. Norris's last letters, you will immediately proceed to break up all mining operations so far as we are concerned, and to send Mr. Norris and all the men home that you can dispense with, by the cheapest route consistent with their proper comfort; after which you will proceed to sell the machinery and all the mining property belonging to us in California, taking care not to sell anything for a less amount than will cover costs and charges.

You will, as time and occasion may offer, make enquiries and explorations, to ascertain whether some mine in California may not be obtained where some of the machines can be erected, which

---

* Original in the Beale archives.

will undoubtedly pay well for the expense and trouble of their erection. If some such arrangement as the following could be made we think it would be desirable; that is, if any party should be in possession of a good mine, (which by the way must in the first place be thoroughly examined by yourself, Rube and Hart), and are disposed to go to the expense of the transportation and erection of machinery, it will be well to arrange with them if you can make sufficiently favorable terms, such for instance as these:

The cost and charges of the machines to be put against the mine and transportation and erection of the machinery, and each party to own an undivided half of the mine and machinery. You will perceive that the principal feature of any arrangement you may see fit to make, must be to relieve us, as far as possible, from any additional outlay. You will receive herewith a letter of credit for the purpose of sending our men home if necessary, and to pay other unavoidable expenses.

We think this letter, in connection with the full conversations we have had with you on the subject, will be sufficient to put you in possession of our views on these important matters, and we look with confidence to your promptness and decision to put an end, as soon as practicable, to all our expenses there as far as Gold mining is concerned, and that you may in your own living and explorations, as well as those whom you may employ, steadily practice those notions of rigid economy, which you have learned and practiced in your excursions over the mountains. You well know we cannot afford either you or the men more than a mere living until we shall be in receipt of some returns from your operations. You will be careful to lose no opportunity of correspondence with us. Wishing you health, happiness and success in your contemplated enterprise, we remain,

Your friends,

And Obt Servts

R. L. STOCKTON
G. W. ASPINWALL

Lt E. F. BEALE
 U. S. Navy

With this in view, Beale resigned his commission in May, 1851, and he and his wife went to live in California. Here his extraordinary business ability was manifested at once. The first tour of inspection of the gold mines convinced him of the ultimate value of these properties, but years were needed to develop them, and in the meantime there was a more pressing necessity for immediate returns. He thereupon devised an ingenious way of coping with the situation. Gold-seekers en route to California required one thing more than anything else, namely, transportation, and were willing to pay handsomely for it. So Beale created a transport service, using the personnel of the mines and ranches under his control. In less than a year he cleared a hundred thousand dollars for his principals, who had not expected a substantial return for a much longer time.

Beale's knowledge of the country and frontier problems, combined with his high personal standing, led to his appointment by President Fillmore as General Superintendent of Indian Affairs for the states of California and Nevada. This was in 1852, when he was but thirty years old. The appointment carried with it an appropriation of $250,000 for the protection and colonization of the Indian tribes, and such wide administrative powers that it was described as "vice-regal in breadth and scope and finality."

Beale, who had come East just before the appointment, was now directed to return by the shortest route and survey the choice of lands for Indian reservations. He set out with a party of twelve persons, including a distant relative of his own, named Gwinn Harris Heap, and two members of the Riggs family of Washington. This trip across the plains in '53 became widely known through the publication of an account of the expedition the following year, based on the journals kept by Beale and Heap. It was accompanied by a series of engravings with the title: "Beale Exploration of Central Route to Pacific. Expedition of 1853." There are many interesting details of the party's experiences en route, of which the following may be quoted:

"Yearly expeditions are fitted out in New Mexico to trade with the Pah-Utahs for their children, and recourse is often had to foul means to force their parents to part with them. So common is it to make a raid for this purpose, that it is considered as no more objectionable than to go on a buffalo or a mustang hunt. One of our men, José Gallengo, who was an old hand at this species of man-hunting, related to us, with evident gusto, numerous anecdotes on this subject; and as we approached the village, he rode up to Lieut. Beale and eagerly proposed to him that we should "charge on it like h—ll, kill the *mans,* and maybe catch some of the litle boys and *gals.*" It is scarcely necessary to add that the proposal was rejected.

In the field of Indian affairs, Beale was a true pioneer. The conquest of the West had endowed the national government with a permanent problem, what to do with thousands of primitive people who had been deprived of their means of livelihood, and it was imperative to formulate some kind of policy in regard to them. By taking a census of the Indian population in his area, Beale found that he had seventy thousand wards. They were steadily "melting away" in numbers; he estimated that fifteen thousand or more had died of starvation the preceding winter. The impoverished Indians had little to look forward to except revolt or extermination; indeed, many whites openly advocated an extermination policy. Beale was one of the first Indian administrators in the country to grasp the magnitude of the problem and to propose a practical solution. His experiment was so successful that its adoption on a nationwide scale was immediately proposed. It was described as follows by the Chairman of the Senate Committee on Indian Affairs:

"The moment he became satisfied that if the present order of things were permitted to long continue the results would be disastrous, he tried on a limited scale the plan which I now propose should be generally adopted. He congregated around him upon a small reservation a number of Indians, without interfering in the rights of property or occupancy of any citizen of California. Over one thousand of this simple tribe of Indians, who are mild in their character, not wild like the Comanches or other tribes east of the Sierra Nevada, have flocked around him as their only protector from the misery by which they are surrounded and from the cruel persecution by which they are pursued. Gen. Beale finds these simple people anxious for work, and easily adapting themselves to the changed condition of their affairs. Indeed, such has been the extended success of the experiment, which he undertook on his own responsibility, that hundreds of other Indians are absolutely importuning him to place them under his immediate protection and allow them to work and to live.

86

"There can be no doubt about the success of the experiment upon the scale it has been tried. All observers agree in this favorable verdict, and so encouraged, all the Superintendent of the Indians asks is to be allowed a sufficient amount of money to extend the same system all over California. In this way it is believed that the entire Indian population can be congregated into small districts of country, which will not interfere with any existing white settlements, and which can be protected from incursions. It is supposed that two hundred and fifty thousand dollars will suffice to carry out the plan. If the system is worth anything, and I think it will be successful once it is put into operation, it will be self-sustaining.

"Not only have we reason to expect this but I am assured by General Beale, and we all know he is a practical man, that not only will the system prove self-sustaining but it will prove a useful auxiliary in reducing the expenses of the regular Army Quartermaster's Department in that country. I have not entered into details because we have I am sure implicit confidence in the Superintendent and propose to let him carry out the details of his own plan in his own way."

During his term as Superintendent of Indian Affairs from 1852 to 1856 Beale displayed an extraordinary understanding and humanity toward the peoples under his care. In an age when the rights of the Indians were ruthlessly trampled upon, and the most solemn covenants were cynically violated by the white man, Beale was a just and incorruptible administrator of Indian affairs, and his policy became a model of its kind. When he retired from the post he received from his associates a service of plate bearing this inscription: "Presented to Lieut. Edward F. Beale from those who served under him during his administration of Indian affairs in California. A tribute of affection and respect to one whose plan of Indian civilization was conceived in the purest spirit of philanthropy, pursued with self-sacrificing devotion and energy and crowned with the most pre-eminent success."

VI

A picturesque chapter in the development of the West began in 1854, when camel caravans appeared on the American plains.

After the Mexican War a large territory had been acquired in the Southwest, inhabited mainly by Indians and Mexicans. When the War Department established a chain of Army posts throughout this area it was confronted immediately with a supply problem. The difficulties of transportation brought many suggestions for improvement, including the use of balloons for this purpose. Beale's active and energetic mind searched for a solution. The use of camels was suggested to him by reading E. R. Huc's *Souvenirs d'un voyage dans la Tartarie, le Thibet, et la Chine,* which had been translated by William Hazlitt in 1852. In later years Beale told his son that the idea occurred to him when he was exploring Death Valley with Kit Carson, with the Abbé's book in his saddlebag.

At this time the Secretary of War was Jefferson Davis, later President of the Confederacy. To him Beale presented the idea, fortified by many quotations from travel books to show the camel's usefulness in arid countries. Davis became a fellow-enthusiast, and authorization of the project followed. The Navy provided a ship which was dispatched to the Near East, under the command of Beale's friend and relative, David D. Porter, of later Civil War fame. In Smyrna, Egypt and Tunis some thirty-three camels were purchased and brought back to the United States, and on a second voyage forty-four more. It was Beale's duty to convoy the camels from Texas to California, which he did in 1857. In his official report he commented enthusiastically on the advantages of camels as pack-animals:

"They are the most docile, patient and easily managed creatures in the world, and infinitely more easily worked than mules. From personal observation of the camels I would rather undertake the management of twenty of them than of five mules. In fact the camel gives no trouble whatever. Kneeling down to receive his load, it may be put on without hurry at the convenience of the master, and the process of packing is infinitely easier than mule packing. These animals remain quietly on their knees until loaded. Contrast the lassoing, the blinding, the saddling, the pulling and hauling of ropes, the adjustment of the pack, on an animal like the mule, flying around in all directions, to say nothing of a broken

"The Search for Water"

"The Horses Eagerly Quenching Thirst, Camels Disdaining"

Paintings by Narjot, depicting incidents in the expedition
led by Edward F. Beale in the Southwest to test
camels for use on the American desert

limb received from one of its numerous kicks, with the patient quiet of the camel kneeling for its load.

"We had them on this journey sometimes for twenty-six hours without water, exposed to a great degree of heat, the mercury standing at one hundred and four degrees and when they came to water they seemed to be almost indifferent to it. Not all drank and those that did, not with the famished eagerness of other animals when deprived of water for the same length of time."

They created a furor in California, where most of the inhabitants had never seen a camel. The public reaction may be gauged from a Los Angeles newspaper account:

"Gen. Beale and about fourteen camels stalked into town last Friday week, and gave our streets quite an Oriental aspect. It looks oddly enough to see, outside of a menagerie, a herd of huge, ungainly, awkward but docile animals, move about in our midst, with people riding them like horses. They bring up weird and far-off associations to the Eastern traveller, whether by book or otherwise, of the lands of the mosque, crescent or turban, of the pilgrim mufti and dervish, with visions of the great shrines of the world, Mecca and Jerusalem, and the toiling throngs that have for centuries wended thither; of the burning sands of Arabia and Sahara, where the desert is boundless as the ocean and the camel is the ship thereof.

"These camels under charge of Gen. Beale are all grown and serviceable, and most of them are well broken to the saddle and are very gentle. All belong to the one-hump species, except one which is a cross between the one and the two-hump species. This fellow is much larger and more powerful than either sire or dam. He is a grizzly-looking hybrid, a camel-mule of colossal proportions. These animals are admirably adapted to travel across our continent, and their introduction was a brilliant idea, the result of which is beginning most happily. At first Gen. Beale thought the animals were going to fail; they appeared likely to give out, their backs got sore. But he resolved to know whether they would do or not. He loaded them heavily with provisions, which they were soon able to carry with ease, and thence came through to Fort Tejon, living upon bushes, prickly pears and whatever they could pick up on the route. They went without water from six to ten days and even packed it a long distance for the mules, when crossing the deserts. They were found capable of packing one thousand pounds weight apiece, and of traveling with their load from thirty to forty miles per day, all the while finding their own feed over an almost barren country. Their drivers say they will get fat where a jackass would starve to death. The 'mule,' as they call the cross between the camel and the dromedary, will pack twenty-two hundred pounds."

Undoubtedly the use of camels in the United States would have continued but for the pending outbreak of the Civil War, which eclipsed everything not directly concerned. The difficulties of the experiment were magnified, of course. Many soldiers did not like the animals, and neglect and misuse of the herds took their toll. Some camels wandered away and reverted to a natural state, so that for years afterwards an occasional astonished traveler would behold a wild camel in the distance. Finally an Army board reviewed the camel situation, and brought the experiment to an end. Those remaining were sold at auction, some being purchased by Beale himself for his California ranch.

VII

The fact that Beale was a naval officer in his younger days and subsequently attained the rank of General is sometimes a matter of surprise to those unacquainted with the circumstances of his career. In 1856 the Tulare Indians of California were attacked by a band of whites, and the resulting tension led to widespread fears of an Indian uprising. It was Beale's responsibility to prevent open warfare from breaking out. To give him more authority to cope with the situation, and enable him to control whites as well as Indians, he was appointed Brigadier General in 1856, at the age of thirty-four. The following letter from Major General Wool explains the circumstances of his appointment:

"Being apprehensive that the attack of the white inhabitants on the Tulare Indians, 1856, might lead to an Indian War in Southern California, and from my knowledge of your great efficiency of character and your influence over the Indians in that section of the country, I had no doubt, if employed by the Governor, you would be able to prevent so great a calamity. It was therefore that I not only urged your employment, but, in order that you might more effectually control the whites, especially the Militia, who seemed determined on War against the Indians, I urged upon the Governor your appointment as Brigadier General, which you declined, until urged again and again by myself, which I considered all-important with reference to preserving the peace of the country. When you consented with great reluctance to accept the appointment, the course you adopted and pursued on the occasion referred to, I cannot doubt, settled the difficulties with both whites and Indians."

By this time Beale was playing a decisive role in the development of the West. As his biographer declares, "No step relating to the Pacific Coast was taken or even considered in Washington without consulting him." The greatest problem of the moment was that of new routes to the West. With an immense sectional conflict impending, it was vitally necessary for the Federal Government to establish new communication routes to the Pacific, in order to link the Western territories more firmly to the Union. Beale's explorations now took on an overwhelming importance. It was not merely a question of discovering new roads but of unifying the territory for the impending struggle. That the Far West did not secede from the Union, and thus imperil further the continued existence of the nation, was due in large measure to the work of men like Beale.

When the creation of a new wagon road was decided upon, General Beale was appointed to make the preliminary survey to establish the route. During the summer of 1857 he led a party from Fort Defiance to the Colorado River. His report, dated from the Colorado River, October 16, 1857, was transmitted to Congress, and records the complete success of his mission.

The party left Zuñi, the starting point of the projected route, and reached California in forty-eight days. He reported that the road was "The shortest from our western frontier by 300 miles." The road was nearly level and almost directly west. For the greater part it was well supplied with water, timber and grass. The climate he found healthy, there being no sickness in the party en route. The route crossed the desert at its narrowest point. Other advantages were that the country abounded in game, and Indians were not numerous. The road was passable at all times of the year, and offered emigrants the choice of proceeding directly to Los Angeles, or of turning northward toward San Francisco.

He did not fail to mention the part played by his prized camels. "Our admiration for them," he said, "has increased day by day." He emphasized "their entire adaptation and usefulness in the exploration of the wilderness." He added that he had "subjected them to the trials which no other animal could possibly have endured," and they had proved their worth. He concluded that even a poor camel was worth more than any four of the best mules.

General Beale's report to the Secretary of War, along with his Journal of the expedition, were printed by resolution of the Senate. The Journal is an invaluable account of the conditions of Western exploration during this period. It describes the progress of the party across the preciously little-known country, along with the return journey begun January 1st of the following year. The Journal concludes:

"Here my labors end. A year in the wilderness ended! During this time I have conducted my party from the Gulf of Mexico to the shores of the Pacific Ocean, and back again to the eastern terminus of the road, through a country for a great part entirely unknown, and inhabited by hostile Indians, without the loss of a man. I have tested the value of the camel, marked a new road to the Pacific, and travelled four thousand miles without an accident."

This feat was followed by another exploration that began in the fall of 1858, this time a journey across the 35th parallel. The purpose of the expedition was to prove that winter was no barrier to overland travel in the West. During a winter of "uncommon severity" the party made its way across the plains from Fort Smith, Arkansas, to the Colorado River. Again the leader's report to the Secretary of War announced complete success. Exposure to the weather caused no illness in the party. The route was found to be plentifully supplied "with the three great requisites for overland road—wood, grass and water." He described in detail the character of the countryside that made it suitable for an overland route.

Attached to his report was an estimate of the cost of constructing a railroad from Fort Smith to San Felipe, New Mexico. The total amount he placed at $21,391,100. With his foresight he realized that national wagon roads would soon be supplanted by the coming of the Iron Horse. Over and above the practical value of transcontinental rail connections was the dominant consideration of linking the nation together politically. A contemporary correspondent of the Philadelphia *Press* wrote:

"Ever since the treaty of Guadalupe Hidalgo gave us our California possessions, the same motive that actuates England to draw her Indian colonies to her by lessening the distance and shortening the length of travel between them and the mother country, and that also impels France to desire a ship canal across the Isthmus of Suez, has induced speculations and explorations for a railway route across the continent . . . The public mind has become fully awakened to the importance, in a military as well as commercial point of view, of a railway between the Atlantic and the Pacific. The large majority of the people of the United States are undoubtedly in favor of some route, but the particular route to be selected is the question at issue. This route, beyond all cavil, is that laid down and traveled by Lieut. Beale."

On this overland journey, Beale's return was delayed slightly by an untoward incident, as he reported in a letter to his wife:

Los Angeles,
May 17th, 1859.

My darling Wife,

I arrived here day before yesterday, and shall leave for the Rancho tomorrow. Remaining there a week I shall then return to the Colorado and commence my homeward journey and hope to reach Chester in the month of September. So far our journey has been one of remarkable success, and I anticipate equal good fortune on our return. Unfortunately the troops under Colonel Hoffman in returning from the Colorado robbed our caches of provisions, which will delay me three months.

You know what a cache is? Anything hidden is a *cache*, and I had ordered Bishop to cache for me at the river sufficient to carry me back to New Mexico, which would have enabled me to start back on the 1st of May for home. These soldiers under Colonel Hoffmann robbed the caches, which I believe is the only distinction they have gained in the bloodless campaign from which they have just returned.

93

They made a Treaty with the Indians right upon the ground stained with the blood of the emigrants of whom I have written you in previous letters. Within twenty steps of the place where Hoffman with his thousand men made this treaty, we saw sticking in the rough bark of the trees the golden hair of a child whose brains the bloody savages had knocked out, and picked up the collar bone of a girl wth the string of glass beads she had worn still attached to it.

The very blood stained leaves called for vengeance, but the gallant Colonel having marched his thousand men to the ground marched them back again.

I knew nothing of all this Treaty business and came near spoiling it for them. The day before I got to the river I picked out thirty of our best men, and took them on foot over the mountains intending to come upon the rascals by surprise. We marched rapidly from daybreak until evening, so rapidly that on foot we made thirty miles over mountains in six hours. We came to the river and our men were already on the trail of the Indians, when to our surprise, two white men came up from below and informed us that the troops were at the river, and had encamped at "Beales Crossing" where they had made a Treaty with the Indians.

The next day I moved my whole camp over to the river, and the soldiers having stolen my provisions, I came on into this place to get more.

And now I hear little Trux say, "Well, father has not kept his promise to avenge the poor little children he told us of in his other letter." Now, Truxie, for a story Father has for you of what happened before he got to the river. It is such a good joke you must laugh at it all day. Well, away back in the mountains, two days travel from the river, in a deep ugly ravine filled with huge rocks, when Father was asleep at noon, and the sun hot and clear, the guard ran in and gave the alarm of Indians, and when we went out, sure enough, the rascals had fired at the camp guard, killed one mule dead, wounded another and captured a third.

Then Father and Bishop were terribly frightened, so much so that as soon as it was dark they hitched up all their teams, and horses, and mules, and camels, and fled to the plains a mile or two off, out of the ugly ravine, and built big fires. Then the cruel Indians laughed, and said in the morning they would come and kill us all, that we were cowardly and in the morning they would go and have a fine feast on the mule they had killed, and pick up all we had left in our camp when we ran away. But see, my son, how Providence punishes the wicked. In the early morning the Indians came bounding down the rocks of the ravine shouting and screaming and running to our deserted camps, and when they came to the dead mule, they all set up a great shout to see the dreadful wound that had killed it. Somehow they never quite got through with that shout, for fifteen men ran from the rocks not six feet from them, and fifteen deadly rifles took up the Indian yell and a sharper echo filled the mountain side, and scalps, and bows, and arrows, and spears, and Indian arms were dog cheap in Father's camp before the sun was an hour high. Every story should have its moral, and the moral of this is "Never count your chickens before they are hatched." There now, what do you think of that for a story, and these were the very rascals and at the very spot where Father killed two of them going over winter before last, and just where the poor little girl went to sleep, when the devils were driving the poor emigrants before them.

From Bishop I get the most encouraging news of the Rancho. He says we will have more money than we know what to do with in a year or two more. I find many friends here all glad to see me. A day or two ago I dined with Judge Ozier. His house and grounds are decidedly the best in the State of California. They would be considered beautiful anywhere in the United States. He is nearly blind, the effect I am told of his excesses. What I have seen of him however is not worse than usual.

I suppose Harry is off for Fort Smith long before now, as I received letters from the Department dated Feb. 18th informing me that the money had been placed to my credit in New York for the bridges and road $75,000 and Harry of course was only waiting for that to go on with the work. Copy this paragraph which follows, and send it him; if he is at home read it to him.

If the estimates are too small to admit of the contractors making a reasonable profit, let two or three of the bridges be dropped and the amount applied to the others so as to have the work well done.

The overland mail has just arrived and it gives me but a moment to close my letter, as it goes out immediately.

I am writing near the window, and as the mail draws rattling up to the door I hear some one say "Hello Fred," from which I conclude Mr. Kerlin has come a passenger in it from the Tejon to meet us at this place. Yes, here he is. The first letter I open is from Harry, telling me he is still in Washington and the money

not deposited. His information <u>is incorrect.</u> I have the letter of
the Auditor telling me the Treasury Department has this day
Feby. 16th (1859) placed to my credit on account of the wagon
road appropriation $75,000.

And following this I have the letter of the Assistant Treasurer
at New York Mr. Cisco telling me he had received the money on
Feby. 18th 1859, yet Harry's letters in March complain that
nothing has yet been done. Write him the paragraph as I cannot
write by this mail and it is important he should get the information.

Love to all and kisses to the children,

Your affectionate husband,

E. F. Beale

Mrs. E. F. Beale,
Chester, Pa.

VIII

The Civil War issue now overshadowed all other considerations
in the West. For the North it was vital to maintain the allegiance
of the Pacific Coast area, particularly California. But in
California there were large numbers of Southern sympathizers,
and the position of that state in the forthcoming conflict was by
no means certain. The well-organized Southerners were
determined to secure the secession of California, and contemporary
opinion conceded that this was a strong possibility. When Lincoln
was inaugurated in 1861 his concern for the situation in the West
led to the immediate appointment of officials who could be counted
upon to rally California for the Union.

One of the first of these was the appointment of General Beale
in 1861 as Surveyor General of the states of California and Nevada.
The title that he bore was scarcely a suitable reflection of his
duties and responsibilities, as subsequent events indicated.
Immediately upon taking this office General Beale set about the
real work that it involved, namely, the rallying of the Northern
party to block the danger of secession by California. No one in the
state played a more vital role in the crisis that followed.

The crisis came at once. Lincoln issued a call for a draft of
troops in all loyal states. When the President's proclamation

96

reached California it caused consternation among the Union leaders. Owing to the unsettled situation then prevailing, the attempt to draft Californians into the army would have alienated large sections of the population, perhaps throwing California into the ranks of seceding states. At this critical juncture General Beale took a decisive and successful step. Acting on his own initiative, he boldly suppressed the President's proclamation. The reasons for this unprecedented action he conveyed to Washington in very vigorous terms. Such an action was not without personal danger to himself, but he was guided foremost by his judgment of national welfare. In this he was fully vindicated by the events that followed. President Lincoln commended him for this step, and on Beale's dispatch he wrote the words:

"Draft suspended in California until General Beale shall indicate that the times are more auspicious."

It was a happy solution. Without the draft, Californians volunteered in large numbers, proportionately more than in many other states. The crisis in state affairs was avoided and the Unionists became more powerful. Ultimately California remained with the Union.

Despite the importance of his role in helping to preserve the West for the Union, General Beale desired active service with fighting troops. Accordingly, he wrote the President and volunteered his services in any capacity. His letter gave his reasons as follows:

San Francisco, Cal.,

July 24, 1861.

His Excellency President Lincoln:

A short time ago you did me the honor to appoint me to a most important and responsible position for which I beg you to accept my grateful acknowledgment. Under any other condition of public affairs, you have left me nothing to desire; but to the flag under which I have received honorable wounds, under which my father and my grandfather fought for the honor and the glory of the country, I think I owe something more, in this hour of trial, than a mere performance of duty in a position of ease and quiet. To the government I owe early education and support, for I entered its service almost a child and feel toward it a filial affection and gratitutde. All that I have, even my life I owe to it, and it is a debt I am willing gratefully and cheerfully to discharge.

From fourteen to twenty-five my life was passed at sea, and for the past fifteen years principally on the great plains and in the Rocky Mountains. I served during the Mexican War, and at its close I resigned and have been engaged since in many expeditions of some importance. I know that I am resolute, patient, and active and if I had not courage, my love of country would supply the want of it in such a time as this. Devoted to my country, and owing it everything I have in the world, I write to offer my services to you in any capacity you may wish to use them until the present rebellion is crushed out of the land. You cannot add to the distinction you have already conferred upon me by any appointment, for there is none within your gift more distinguished or more honorable; nor do I desire any change except that I may more efficiently serve the United States. In a word, I wish simply to offer my life for the flag.

With great respect, your obedient servant,

E. F. Beale

In view of the necessity of keeping the West loyal to the Union, Lincoln decided that Beale's most effective service would be rendered by remaining in California. Naturally Beale bowed to his wishes and remained at his post, redoubling his vigilance to aid the Union cause.

Another vital matter at this time was the crowning of Maximilian as Emperor of Mexico. When the Mexicans rose in revolt against this foreign domination they needed arms and ammunition. In sympathy with this liberal uprising General Beale offered his services to arrange the export of desperately needed supplies to the Mexican popular army. The nature of Beale's services in this connection are indicated in the following letter from the Mexican General Vega:

The Path of Empire

Excellency:

In the many conferences which we have had with reference to the French Invasion and the firm resolve of the Constitutional Government to fight to the last extremity to defend the nationality and independence of our country, it has given me very great pleasure to see the interest and the sympathy with which you have followed the heroic efforts of my Fatherland in the defence of the most sacred of causes.

Of course nothing less was to be expected from a worthy general of the Republic, nourished and fortified in the doctrines of Liberty and in the rights of man, or from one who also understands how dangerous it would be for the political principles in the worship of which we are coreligionists, to permit the development on the American Continent of the monarchial principle that the party of European Reaction pretends and seeks to promulgate.

Holding as I do these views, the generous offers which you have been kind enough to make, of your services for the purpose of expediting the export of arms and munitions which have been gathered in this city, compel the deepest gratitude of my countrymen, and of the Constitutional Government, and I for my part am pleased to be called upon to voice this sentiment in which I participate in the highest degree.

I accept, then, the good disposition you have shown in favor of my country's cause, and leave entirely to your loyalty and good faith all the arrangements for the departure of the munitions and arms from this state that may seem to you most convenient, in the understanding however that I will personally embark on the ship with them.

The munitions referred to are now deposited in the warehouses of the government, and also in those of private individuals. In the same way they should be sent out to the Colorado, consigned to the person you may see fit to designate.

At the first opportunity I shall place in your hands the receipts and all the papers relative to the consignment, so that you may arrange the freight and indeed all other questions which their export may entail. I also beg to inform you for your guidance that I will bring on board with me very excellent pilots of the coasts

---

* Translated from the Spanish original, in the Beale archives.

in question, whom I have recruited in advance for the greater security of our landing.

The well-deserved influence and consideration which you enjoy in the official and all respectable circles in this city, and in the other states of the Union, procure for you facilities to render important services to my country such as no one else could; for this reason and because I am convinced that your party has sympathy for our cause and the good will to aid us to sustain it, I do not impress upon you the fact that the actual circumstances of the Constitutional Government of Mexico demands the greatest economy in the purchase of arms, although they are so urgently needed. And it is on the score of this very urgency that I suggest to you to select a steamer so that the cargo may the sooner arrive. Even the very moments are indeed precious.

The preceding suggestions should not be construed as instructions for the performance of the mission you have been so kind as to accept. On the contrary I merely submit them to your good judgment, so that you may modify them as you think best, and in order that you may with your perfect knowledge of men and of affairs adopt the means most suitable for carrying out the work we have in hand. In sending this note I have the honor to offer to you the consideration of my particular respect and esteem.

Independence — Liberty — Reform.

San Francisco, May 17th, 1864,

PLACIDO VEGA.

To GEN. E. F. BEALE

Under this arrangement General Beale shipped eight thousand rifles to the Mexicans army under Juarez, and they were used in the decisive battles that followed. Years after the event, Beale was publicly recognized by President Diaz as a benefactor of Mexico.

IX

In May, 1864, Beale terminated his work as Surveyor General, largely owing to his dissatisfaction with the Government's mining policy, which he thought unjust to the miners. In his report of the previous year he suggested remedial steps, such as the adoption

100

of Spanish mining laws, "as the wisest and most liberal." He also proposed a convention to draft a mining code, and advocated the deeding of Federal mining lands to the states and territories. These suggestions were not favored in Washington, for they conflicted with the views of the Interior Department, which Beale thought were prejudicial to the welfare of the West. A somewhat acrimonious dispute followed. Beale stated his case vigorously in a letter "to the people of California" and withdrew, saying that "I never desire again a place in public affairs."

Three years before he had written a friend that "I have been looking forward with the keenest delight to two or three years of rest after so many long ones of hardship." The opportunity now presented itself. General Beale was the owner of an enormous ranch, near what is now the town of Bakersfield, California. To this estate, called Tejon Rancho, he now retired.

In 1857, four years before Beale became Surveyor General, he had purchased Tejon Rancho from Spanish and Mexican absentee landowners, some of whom had little interest in the huge tracts of land they controlled in that part of the country. It was a favorite anecdote of General Beale's in later years that sometimes he had to convince them they actually owned the land before he could buy it. It was a windfall for them when Beale purchased it at five cents an acre. The circumstances of the acquisition of the ranch were described by General Beale some years later to a correspondent of a San Francisco newspaper:

"When, in 1857, I came from Little Salt Lake in Utah via Amargosa," said the General, "and struck this valley at Big Rock, I travelled West to Tejon Pass along the foothills, and was as you can imagine highly impressed with the country. There was considerable grass and wild game, but not a single human being did we see. At Elizabeth Lake the ducks and geese were so thick that I killed three ducks with one shot of my rifle. We did not have shotguns then."

"I bought this forty thousand acre tract and started to raise cattle. In those days my nearest neighbors were at Visalia on one side and at Los Angeles on the other."

There was no one living on the place, and the only building was a deserted fort, but General Beale rapidly transformed it into a flourishing cattle ranch. Additional land acquisitions made the

General's holdings "half as large as the state of Rhode Island." Lincoln is supposed to have joked with his Surveyor General about becoming "monarch of all he surveyed," but the story was undoubtedly an invention, for the lands had been acquired before his appointment.

For the best available description of life at the Rancho we are indebted to the novelist Charles Nordhoff, who visited there in 1872, and subsequently dedicated a book to General Beale, "In memory of the pleasant days at Tejon." Nordhoff wrote:

"Our host was a sparkling combination of scholar, gentleman and Indian fighter, the companion and friend of Kit Carson in other days, the surveyor of trans-continental railways and wagon roads and the owner today of what seems to me the most magnificent estate in a single hand in America.

"The Rancho from which I write, the Tejon as it is called, the home of Gen. Beale, contains nearly two hundred thousand acres and lies at the junction of the Sierra Nevada with the Coast Range. These two mountain ranges bend around toward each other here in a vast sweep and form the bottom of the San Joaquin Valley. They do not quite meet. The Tejon Pass, a narrow defile, separates them and gives egress from the Valley into the Los Angeles country.

"You may ride for eighty miles on the county road upon this great estate. It supports this year over one hundred thousand sheep; and it has a peasantry of its own about whom I shall tell you something presently. The Tejon is devoted to sheep, and here I saw the operation of shearing; eight or nine weeks are required to shear the whole flock, as well as the various details of the management of a California sheep farm.

"What we call at home a flock is in California called a band of sheep. These bands consist usually of from 1,300 to 2,000 sheep, and each band is in the charge of a shepherd.

" 'This country is quiet now,' said the General one evening in a reminiscent mood, 'but when I first came into it it contained some rough people. The head of the famous robber Joaquin Murieta and the hand of his lieutenant, "Three-fingered" Jack, were brought into my camp but a few hours after those two scoundrels were shot. Jack Powers and his gang used to herd their bands of stolen horses on my ranch as they drove them through the country; and Jack once kindly came to tell me that he would kill the first man of his gang that took anything from me. Mason and Henry, the worst of all the road agents in this state, used to go through Kern County waylaying and robbing; and in those days a man had to be careful not only of his money but of his life.'

"Of course the sheep are scattered over many miles of territory, but each band has a limited range, defined somewhat by the vicinity of water, and it is customary in California to drive them every night into a corral or inclosure, usually fenced with brush and with a narrow entrance. This corral is near water and the sheep drink at morning and evening. The shepherd sleeps near by, in a hut, or, in the mountainous part of the Tejon Rancho, in a *tepestra*. The corral is to keep the sheep together, and in a measure protect them against the attacks of wild beasts, which, curiously enough are too cowardly to venture after dark inside of even a low fence. The *tepestra* is to protect the shepherd himself against the attacks of grizzly bears which are still abundant in the mountains, especially in the Coast Range.

"The *tepestra* is a platform about 12 feet high, built upon stout poles solidly set into the ground. On this platform the shepherd sleeps, in the mountains, at the entrance to the corral; the grizzly bear cannot climb a pole, though he can get up a tree large enough to give his claws a hold. It is, I believe, not infrequent for a grizzly to stand up at the side of a *tepestra* at night and try to rouse the shepherd. But all the men are armed with guns, which they carry day and night.

"The grizzly does not usually attack sheep. The California lion, a very strong but cowardly beast, the wildcat, the fox and the coyote, are the sheep's enemies. The last named is easily poisoned with meal which has strychnine powdered over it. The others are hunted when they become troublesome, and as the lion upon the slightest alarm will take to a tree, and will run even from a small dog, it is not accounted a very troublesome beast.

"Indians, Spaniards, Chinese, and some Scotchmen, serve as shepherds in California. The last are thought the best, and the Chinese make very faithful shepherds, if they are properly and carefully trained. They are apt to herd the sheep too closely together at first. Dogs I have found but little used in the sheep ranches I have seen. They are not often thoroughly trained, and where they are neglected become a nuisance. Of course the shepherds have to be supplied at stated intervals with food. They usually receive a week's rations which they cook for themselves.

"At the Tejon there are two supply stations, and every morning donkeys and mules were sent out with food to some distant shepherds. The ration-masters count the sheep as they deliver the rations, and thus all the sheep are counted once a week and if any sheep are missing they must be accounted for. The shepherd is allowed to kill a sheep once in so many days but he must keep the pelt which is valuable. Above the ration-masters are the major-domos. Each of these has charge of a certain number of bands; on a smaller estate there is usually but one major-domo. It is his duty to see that the shepherds are competent; that new pasturage is ready when a band has need for it; to see that the corrals are in good order; to provide extra hands at lambing time; to examine the sheep, to keep out scab which is almost the only disease sheep are subject to in this State; and to give out the rations for distribution.

"On such an estate as the Tejon there is finally a general superintendent and a bookkeeper and a storekeeper, for here in the wilderness a supply of goods of various kinds must be kept up for the use of the people. A blacksmith, teamsters, plowmen, gardeners and house servants make up the complement of the Tejon's company. The gardeners and servants are Chinese as they usually are in this State, and very good men they are—civil, obliging, and competent.

"Besides these numbers fed from the home place there are on this estate about 300 Indians, who have been allowed to fence in small tracts of land, on which they raise barley and other provisions, and in some cases plant fruit trees and vines. They form the peasantry of whom I spoke above, and are a happy, tolerably thrifty, and very comfortable people. Their surplus produce is purchased by the superintendent; when their labor is used they are paid; and they all have horses which pasture on the general fields. They have learned how to plow, shear sheep, and perform some other useful labor.

"Now these Indians came to the Tejon naked, except a breech clout, feeding miserably on grasshoppers, worms and acorns, ignorant, savage nomads. They were first brought here when a part of this rancho was used by the Government as an Indian Reservation. Gen. Beale, the present owner of the Tejon, was then Superintendent of Indian Affairs in this State, and he has seen these people emerge from a condition of absolute barbarism and wretchedness into a degree of comfort and prosperity greater than that enjoyed by the majority of Irish peasants; they have abandoned their nomadic habits, have built neat and comfortable houses and fenced in ground which they cultivate. Their women dress neatly and understand how to cook food. The men earn money as sheep shearers. In some places vineyards and fruit trees have been brought by them to a bearing condition. In short these human beings were savages, and are—well, they are as civilized as a good many who come in emigrant ships from Europe to New York.

"And all this has been accomplished under the eye and by the careful and kindly management of the owner of the Tejon Rancho. It seemed a great thing for any man to achieve, and certainly these people compared in every way favorably with a similar class whom I saw on the Tule River Indian Reservation, living at the expense of the Government, idle, gambling, lounging, evil-eyed and good for nothing. . . . Gen. Beale's Indians have been raised to a far better condition by his own private efforts, than the Reservation Indians after years of expensive support from the Government."

At the Tejon, General Beale wrote occasionally on various subjects that interested him, political and otherwise. Among his writings was a tribute to his old friend of pioneer days, Kit Carson. A well-known poem entitled "Kit Carson's Ride," by Joaquin Miller, aroused him to wrath because of its many inaccuracies of fact and character, and inspired him to write a lengthy reply that recalled some of the leading incidents of Carson's career.

X

Shortly after the Civil War, General Beale purchased Decatur House to serve as his home in Washington. Owing to its wartime use the house was then in a state of disrepair, and required extensive renovation. Among other things, new flooring was laid in the drawing rooms, of California woods inlaid with the arms of the state. When the renovation of the house was completed, he furnished it in the early General Grant taste of the period.

One day while the work was in progress a lady called who expressed the desire to go through the house. General Beale protested that the rooms were filled with bricks, plaster and mortar, and could not be shown at that time. Then she requested to see the drawing rooms, at least.

"Certainly," he said, "if you will excuse the condition of the house." He escorted her up the stairway, and when the lady entered the rooms she burst into tears. Recovering her composure, she said with evident embarrassment, "Where we are now standing I was married, and here the happiest days of my life were spent. I was Cora Livingston. My father occupied the house when he was Secretary of State. I am Mrs. Barton, a widow, and I came here to buy this house."

Sympathetically the General explained that Decatur House was not for sale; indeed, he had given it to his wife at the time of purchase. The lady thanked him for his courtesy and departed.

From about 1870 on, General Beale and his wife divided their time between Decatur House and the Tejon. In Washington the General rapidly became one of the outstanding leaders of social and political life. His friend Grant had just been elected to the Presidency, and Beale was the most trusted member of the inner Presidential circle. He was also named president of the National Republican League, and was a key figure in the party politics of the era.

Beale had first met Grant in Mexico City while en route across Mexico with the news of the gold discovery in California. Their friendship, however, began five years later in San Francisco, in 1853, at a time when Grant believed his Army career was over. "In those days," says Beale's biographer, "when Grant was unfortunate, Beale stood by his friend with both word and deed. They walked the Long Wharf together and ate their meals at the 'What Cheer House,' when San Francisco was as uncertain of its name as of its future."

Following Grant's great Civil War career he was elected President in 1868. Up to this time he had cared little for politics, and had voted but once in his life—for the Democratic ticket. Under the circumstances he had need of friends and advice. "Grant had the gift of friendship, and his circle was not small; but to the Washington of the seventies it was no secret that of all his personal friends the one he most admired, the one to whom he always listened (and then did as his own good sense dictated) was 'Ned' Beale."

The President spent much time at Decatur House, informally, in the evenings. In later years the General's son, Truxtun Beale, would tell how he was delegated by his father to sit up with General Grant while the elder Beale went to bed. It seemed that Grant

Decatur House about 1880, after Edward Beale had added
Victorian trimming to the facade

liked late hours, and would sit up smoking and drinking endless tankards of ale.

President Grant in 1876 appointed General Beale as Envoy Extraordinary and Minister Plenipotentiary to the court of Austria-Hungary. The appointment was very popular, particularly in California, where Beale was regarded as a native son. An indication of this enthusiasm is shown in the comment by the San Francisco *News Letter:*

"The news of Ned Beale's appointment to be Minister to Austria, succeeding Mr. John Jay, is as refreshing as a shower of rain—for if ever there was a typical and representative Californian, Ned Beale is he. Setting out in life a Lieutenant in the Navy, he had a chance to fight in the Territorial days and he fought like the devil. Appointed to look after the Arizona Indians at a time when Arizona Indians were at their best and meanest, he polished them off and taught them to stand around in such style that they have never been the same Indians since.

"Those were days when Indians were Indians, and their only use for a Commissioner was to scalp him on sight. In his Arizona administration Beale took bigger risks, showed more endurance, underwent more trying hardships than any other man, whether in the Army or out of it. He outscouted any scout and out-rode any mail-rider we had in the service. He showed himself an iron man put up with steel springs and whalebone, and all this time, be it noted, he was only a youngster.

"Finally, the war came and Beale went Union, and got thereby the Surveyor - Generalship of California. Ned Beale was no sentimentalist—not by the longest kind of odds. He was born with a head on his shoulders, was Edward, and he never laid it away in his trunk."

In accepting a position as Minister at the court of Vienna, General Beale knew that diplomatic skill of a high order would be expected of him. The reigning Emperor had helped his favorite brother, Maximilian, to become Emperor of Mexico. Then the Mexican revolt under Juarez, with American assistance, led to Maximilian's death. This severely strained American relations with Vienna. More than this, General Beale himself had supported and supplied guns to the rebels. It was evident that General Beale's appointment would place him in a difficult and exacting position.

However, he accepted the assignment and departed at once

for Vienna, where he presented himself at the Court. He was received by the Emperor with every courtesy, and with as much cordiality as could be expected under the circumstances. A few days later, Beale had his first conference with Count Jules Andrassy, head of the Foreign Office, who brought up the subject of Mexico. With bold frankness General Beale stated the facts in full, disdaining to modify any aspect of the situation. His candor made a favorable impression upon Andrassy, who commended him to the Emperor.

"General Beale," he reported to the Emperor, "is the only man who has ever made the Mexican tragedy clear to me. You should speak with him."

As a result of this favorable impression, General Beale was summoned to the royal palace of Schoenbrunn for private audience with the Emperor. Then and in subsequent months General Beale succeeded in dissipating the coolness that he first encountered. Being an accomplished horseman, he was often invited on hunts by the Empress Elizabeth. It was a personal triumph for him that he overcame the difficulties of an awkward situation and established cordial and friendly relations with the court of the Dual Monarchy.

With his pressing business affairs at home, General Beale had no desire for a protracted career in the diplomatic service. A year in Vienna had given him a sufficient taste of the glamor of a foreign court, and he desired to return to Washington. Accordingly he sent in his resignation. The Secretary of State thanked him for services in improving American relations with the court of Vienna.

That same year Grant left the White House and began a series of extended travels. During the time he corresponded extensively with his friend General Beale, opening his heart to him as he did to no one else. This correspondence, which continued until the President's death in 1885, forms an invaluable part of the record of Grant's later life.* Some of it was published subsequently as a "memorial of a friendship" that lasted more than fifty years.

These letters provide some intimate, charming glimpses of the personality and outlook of the great commander. The following are four hitherto unpublished letters from this correspondence:

---

* Originals in the Beale archives.

PHOTOGRAPH IN DECATUR HOUSE OF THE EMPRESS ELIZABETH OF AUSTRIA,
GIVEN TO EDWARD F. BEALE WHILE MINISTER TO THAT COUNTRY
(Probably hitherto unpublished)

THE AMERICAN LEGATION IN VIENNA AND STATE CARRIAGE WAITING TO TAKE THE
MINISTER, EDWARD F. BEALE, FOR AN AUDIENCE WITH THE EMPEROR FRANZ JOSEF

PHOTOGRAPH OF MARY EDWARDS BEALE, WIFE OF EDWARD F. BEALE,
TAKEN IN VIENNA WHILE HE WAS UNITED STATES
MINISTER TO AUSTRIA-HUNGARY, 1876-77

PHOTOGRAPH OF MARY BEALE BAHKMÉTEFF, WIFE OF LAST IMPERIAL RUSSIAN
AMBASSADOR, GEORGE BAHKMÉTEFF, IN WASHINGTON, 1911-17.
SHE IS DRESSED IN RUSSIAN COURT ROBES

The Path of Empire

Paris, France,
October 6th, 1878.

My dear General:

We have now been in Paris for nearly two weeks and are getting ready for our journeying again. This time we go to Spain, Portugal and a little of Africa, bordering on the Mediterranean and Atlantic. This time we will settle down for the winter probably in Paris though possibly in the south of France or Italy. I received your last letter some time ago, while in Vienna I think. I found Vienna one of the most beautiful cities in Europe. But everybody retires so horribly early. After ten at night the streets are as silent as the grave.

I hope your diplomacy will prove successful in bringing over the Arabian steeds.* I have heard nothing however. By accident we have not yet met Mrs. Bakhmeteff.** She did not learn of our arrival until we had been here a week and then when she did call both Mrs. Grant and myself were out. I believe she is well, however, and hope Mrs. Grant will see a good deal of her yet before we start. The weather has been very fine since our last arrival in Paris, the first good weather I have ever seen here for any number of consecutive days. But I would like to swap off the balance of this week to be with you visiting the farm, out looking at the colts. I hope the latter are doing well and that they will not disappoint you.

If you see Dan Ammen tell him that I have entirely abandoned the idea of going around the world. Certainly or unless I should conclude to remain absent another year which I think entirely improbable. Mrs. Grant joins me in kindest regards to Mrs. Beale, Miss Emily and yourself.

Very truly yours,

U. S. Grant.

Gen. E. F. Beale.

---

* The Arab stallions "Leopard" and "Linden Tree," presented to General Grant by the Sultan of Turkey.

** Mary, eldest daughter of E. F. Beale, and wife of Russian diplomat, George Bakhmeteff.

Paris, Jan. 17th, 1879.

Dear General:

I am in receipt of your letter of the 4th of Jan. Mr. Borie has not put in an appearance yet, though the papers noted his arrival in Liverpool two or three days ago. We start in the morning for Marseilles to take the French steamer for Alexandria, thence by rail to Suez, thence the P.O. line to Bombay. But as the steamer does not leave Marseilles until the 23d Mr. Borie will have abundance of time to join us. Starting at this time we will be able to do up India while the season is pleasant, and in time to take the Richmond on her arrival at Calcutta. It is impossible for me to fix a time now when I will reach California. If I cannot get to Japan early in May I will probably remain in China until the cool weather in the fall—say the 1st of Oct. In this case I would not reach San Francisco until sometime in Dec. But I shall certainly be in the States before the end of the year barring accidents.

You have seen by the papers that I have just made a run through Ireland. I was only in the northern part. I was much pleased with the people. There are no more thrifty, self reliant and contented people in Europe today than the people of North Ireland. I saw no idle factories and no indication of poverty. Business may not be so brisk or so remunerative as it was during, and directly after our war, but it is on a solid basis.

I anticipate much pleasure from the trip before me, but as I believe I have said to you in a previous letter, I get very homesick some times. I long for a quiet hour.

Give Mrs. Grant's love to Mrs. Beale and Miss Emily and my kindest regards. Tell Ammen that I may not write to him before we get to Bombay, but I am always pleased to hear from him.

My address will continue to be same as before, or to the care of the U.S. Consul either at Bombay or Calcutta. Write to me often.

Very truly yours,

U. S. GRANT.

GEN. E. F. BEALE.

PHOTOGRAPH OF EMILY BEALE (right), DAUGHTER OF EDWARD F. BEALE,
TAKEN WITH EDITH FISH, DAUGHTER OF HAMILTON FISH,
SECRETARY OF STATE

New York City

Dec. 28th 1882.

My dear General Beale:

Unexpectedly to me I shall be going to Washington on Tuesday next to remain I cannot tell how long. Mrs. Grant and I had accepted an invitation from both Cameron and yourself to visit you during the winter. As I am going on business however— connected with framing a Commercial Treaty with Mexico—and will want to consult with Senators, particularly with members of the Committee on Foreign Relations and Commerce, both Mrs. Grant and I think we had better take rooms at a hotel until that business is settled. I think of taking Mrs. Grant's carriage and team as we may be delayed much longer than we now think. I wish I could take mine also which have shown a 2.25 gait with my driving. But this latter I will forego.

With best regards to all your family,

Yours truly,

U. S. GRANT.

Would you advise me to take rooms at the Arlington or where? Please telegraph me. Our stay in Washington may be for a month or more, or the business part of it may be completed in a few days. Of course if we find there is no disposition on the part of the Senate to ratify such a treaty as can be made that will end the matter at once.

U. S. G.

New York, March 2, 1884.

My dear General Beale:

Mrs. Grant and I are very much obliged to you and Mrs. Beale for your kind invitation to stop over at your house on our way to Fortress Monroe, but I would not consent to stop in Washington while in my present condition, unable to walk I would necessarily be confined to my room all the time where I would be accessible to callers and it would overrun the house with people seeking my assistance to procure office as well as people who would call to pay their respects and whom I should be very glad to see. After

111

the receipt of your letter, however, I had a letter written to the President of the Pennsylvania Road to secure a car to take me directly from here to Newport News, and also wrote to the Hygeia Hotel at Old Point to secure rooms.

I have received no answer yet from the Railroad, but have from the Hotel saying I can have the accommodations I want. If I get an answer in time saying that I can have a car I shall leave here on Thursday evening of this week so as to reach Washington in time to connect with the six o'clock train. Mrs. Grant and I are very glad that you and Mrs. Beale and Miss Emily contemplate going with us, and I will telegraph you the moment I learn that I can have a car on time. If it should be later than Thursday before one can be secured I will inform you at the earliest moment on what day and train we leave here.

With kindest regards to you and all your family,

Very truly yours,

U. S. GRANT,

per FRANK F. WOOD.

I expected to have answered your letters last Friday but Buck among the numerous messages that I sent by him that morning, forgot to tell Mr. Wood who writes this letter at my dictation, to come up that day, and the next day being Saturday I concluded it was just as well to wait until Sunday.

During this period the American Navy was undergoing a program of expansion, the building of the new White Squadron, in which General Beale played an advisory role. His interest in naval affairs had continued undiminished throughout the years. "While in Vienna," his biographer writes, "it was said of him that he would travel a thousand miles to avoid an idle function, and twice that distance to visit an interesting navy yard or a stud farm." After General Grant's retirement from the Presidency he urged President Arthur to make Beale Secretary of the Navy, but practical politics led to another choice, and Grant never forgave his successor.

One of the lesser episodes of General Beale's closing years occurred in the historic drawing rooms of Decatur House. For some time Grant had been engaged in a bitter personal feud with a member of his own party, James G. Blaine. In the interests of party harmony Beale had endeavored to reconcile them, but without success. On the eve of the election of 1884, Beale was asked by the party leaders to make another effort. At this time Grant was a guest at Decatur House, while Blaine lived on the opposite side of Lafayette Square. Beale tried again, and was successful in arranging a reconciliation. The subsequent conference of the three men at Decatur House healed the long breach and restored party unity. Blaine was nominated for the Presidency, but lost to Cleveland.

In his later years General Beale retained the vigorous energy that had characterized his life. A newspaper account in 1887 described him as follows: "In appearance General Beale is of short, sinewy stature, of very dark complexion, with a closely-cut mustache and hair almost white. He has a nervous energy in his actions and movements which indicate the high spirit and gallantry which he has shown in all the walks of life, whether in the front of the assaulting column moving on the works of the enemy; in the peaceful pursuits of Indian administration; as pathfinder across the continent; as diplomat at the court of the House of Hapsburg-Lorraine, or in the management of his vast landed possessions." But this health that had served him so well eventually began to fail.

It was not until 1892, however, that he seemed to realize that his active and crowded life was drawing to a close. In April of that year he wrote to his wife, "All the property I have in the world is in your name." By the following Spring he could only dictate this last letter to his son:

"Dear Trux: I wish you to live with your Mother and take care of her and cherish her—remember the devotion she has always shown you. You have done all that I have asked of you and have acquired a well earned high reputation. Enjoy the rest of your life. I do not wish you to go to the ranch. It is a wearing life and Pogson is quite competent to conduct it, and moreover, I want you near your Mother, who will need all your assistance. Go to California occasionally and look into our affairs. That is all that is necessary.

"Goodbye my dear Boy. I have always loved you and been very proud of you.

Your affectionate Father,

E. F. BEALE."*

General Beale died at Decatur House on April 22, 1893, and after simple funeral services in Washington was buried in Chester, Pennsylvania, his wife's home. Messages of condolence were received from the President, from Cabinet members, from Justices, Ambassadors, Congressmen, and from a host of personal friends, as well as from the courts of Vienna, St. Petersburg and Athens. In the American press there were many tributes to his distinguished career, and many recognized his passing as symbolic of the closing of a chapter in American history.

At Tejon Rancho there were tributes as well, of a simpler nature, that showed how General Beale was loved by the people of his own Western lands. Here were two aged Indians who had accompanied the General on many journeys. When Romundo heard the sad news he was incredulous, and as the realization of it came over him he said simply, "I do not care to live any longer." A day later he died. Juan Maravia, "the incomparable packer," was deeply affected when he heard his patron was gone. "I may be able to help him," said the aged Indian, and began to make preparations for a journey. One morning his children found him under the fig tree, but his body was cold.

---

*From Beale archives.

TRUXTUN BEALE.
FROM A PORTRAIT PHOTO BY ARNOLD GENTHE

CHAPTER XI

TRUXTUN BEALE

IN THE opening decades of the twentieth century La Fayette Square became suddenly more conscious of its past when new buildings of modern design invaded the neighborhood. The La Fayette Square Opera House, afterwards a theatre, appeared on the site of the old residence of Commodore Rodgers, which was demolished in 1895. The United States Chamber of Commerce replaced the Corcoran house; the Hay-Adams House, a hotel, the John Hay and Henry Adams residences. By contrast with these newcomers the older buildings clearly belonged to another era. They were now part and parcel of history, which endowed them with an added significance as mementoes of the past.

After being closed for a period following the death of his mother, Decatur House was occasionally reopened after 1903 as the Washington residence of Truxtun Beale, son of Edward Fitzgerald Beale, and former United States Minister to Persia and Greece, Rumania and Serbia, a man of cosmopolitan background and training, popular for his ready wit, genuine kindness, and occasional charming eccentricities. He and his wife, Marie Chase Oge, whom he had just married, continued and preserved the tradition of hospitality in the historic residence on La Fayette Square, accepting it as an obligation to the past as well as to the present.

Each year, after the President's reception, the entire diplomatic corps repaired to Decatur House for the annual supper that was an institution in Washington society. Here the envoys resplendent in uniforms and decorations, and their ladies radiant in silks and jewels, mingled with Cabinet members, Congressmen, judges, publishers and other guiding powers in American political life, and their wives and other distinguished women from many parts of the country. These assemblies, instituted by Mrs. Beale, filled the fine old drawing rooms of Decatur House with a brilliant elegance reminiscent of the Old World. No doubt Stephen Decatur, who had intended these rooms to serve as a center of social life in Washington, would have been gratified at this continued fulfillment of his intention after a lapse of over a century.

Truxtun Beale was an extraordinary product of later nineteenth-century America, combining the advantages of wealth and station with unusual personal energy and talent. He had been born in California, March 6, 1856, during one of his parents' visits to the West, but was educated in the East at Chester Military College, in Pennsylvania. Not content with military training and a degree in civil engineering, he went on to enter Harvard Law School. However, when his father was appointed in 1876 to represent the United States at the court of the Dual Monarchy of Austro-Hungary, Truxtun Beale interrupted his law studies to accompany the Minister to Vienna, as private secretary. On returning to the United States he resumed the study of law at Columbia University, from which he was graduated in 1878, and was admitted to the Pennsylvania bar. Thus at the outset of his career he had the advantages of diversified training, military, engineering, legal and diplomatic.

There followed the customary Grand Tour, which he elected to take in the Orient, travelling mainly in China and Japan. Here he acquired a lifelong interest in the Far East, and a deep appreciation of American responsibilities in that part of the world. Upon his return home he became the manager of his father's California estate, the vast Tejon Rancho, for his father evidently desired him to have practical business experience, particularly in the administration of this estate which he would eventually inherit. So for a number of years Truxtun Beale devoted himself to the management of this semifeudal Western domain. Here some of the old camel bells, engraved with verses from the Koran, were still treasured as reminders of his father's camel experiment some decades before.

He might have entered politics, but the Tejon Rancho kept him too busy for this at first, and he never afterwards had the inclination to do so. Nevertheless he followed political developments closely, in view of his father's close friendship with President Grant. Grant's second term was overshadowed by a financial panic, and he was glad to retire from office in 1877, departing at once on

PHOTOGRAPH OF A SUPPER AT DECATUR HOUSE AFTER THE DIPLOMATIC RECEPTION
AT THE WHITE HOUSE, 1938

Truxtun Beale, son of Edward F. Beale, in uniform of cadet
at Pennsylvania Military Academy, 1867-74, and his
father's body servant, Jordan, a former
slave of William Garrison

a tour of the world. When Grant returned to Washington the following year he was entertained at Decatur House, and visited there frequently until his death in 1885. Of this event, Truxtun Beale wrote at the time:

"I saw General Grant a few days before he died. He had been on terms of intimate friendship with my father, and during many years our house had been his accustomed home whenever he was in Washington. Myself a very young man, I looked upon him with awe as the greatest of military heroes. When he was dying I visited him at Mount McGregor. Somewhat misdoubting the propriety of doing so under the circumstances, I sent in my card. I was admitted, and he received me with that kindness which was so marked a characteristic of the man.

"I was greatly shocked to observe how much he was changed, owing to the ravages of his disease. Though suffering intense pain, and indeed well nigh in the last agony of death, his wasted appearance seemed to bring out the nobility of his features and the kindly expression of his face. Instead of speaking of his own distresses, he first saw that I was comfortable and then asked me about my father. We have all heard how Lord Chesterfield, when he had only a few moments to live, directed his attendant to offer a chair to a visitor; but here was a man, born in the wilderness, with whom courtesy was an instinct. He was so innately a gentleman that in that quality he was the equal of the finest gentleman in Europe, without even being aware of the fact."

In 1891, when Truxtun Beale was thirty-five years of age, President Harrison appointed him Minister to Persia. With his background and training the new Minister was well qualified for the post, and though it was his first diplomatic appointment he was no stranger to the legations. Diplomacy attracted him when politics did not, and he was willing to leave his beloved Tejon Rancho for a term of office in a foreign capital. He proceeded at once to Teheran for a year's service in the vivid and colorful court of the Shah of Persia.

He was fascinated by Persia, and found there an ample field for the exercise of his varied talents. One of his most important Ministerial duties in a backward country was to obtain concessions for American commerce, and he was signally successful. American missionaries in an Islamic area were similarly in need of assistance, and he obtained for them the most important previously-denied privilege, the right to hold property. As a result of this, the grateful missionaries urged him to remain in Persia.

Diplomatic life in a country like Persia was no quiet affair, but contained elements of great excitement and personal danger. A crisis arose when the Shah sold a concession to the British, giving them a tobacco monopoly. The ominous result was described in these words by William C. Fox, First Secretary of the American Legation:

"Instantly the whole country was thrown into turmoil. Hundreds of thousands of families had been engaged for centuries in the national business of growing and handling tobacco. Now their rights had been sold out to dogs of Christians. Ominous growls were heard with every puff of a Persian pipe, and the Shah was prepared with military force to punish in short order what was thought would be a small uprising of the people.

"Then the church came to the rescue. The Persian religion has the strongest hold on the heart of the Islamite. The mullahs, or high priests, wield a power the force of which is marvelous. Only one day had passed when the great mullah of all, the Persian Pope, as it were, came forth with the solemn announcement from the altar of his mosque that, inasmuch as the tobacco of all Persia must now pass through the hands of Christians on its way to the consumer, it was thereby polluted, and no Islamite might smoke it and still be holy.

"It was wondrous, the smashing of kalians that then took place throughout Teheran. Notwithstanding that the use of tobacco is so much a part of the life of all Persians, it is absolutely true that, following the dictum of the great mullah, not a whiff of tobacco was puffed by the faithful in all Teheran, or, as far as I know, all Persia. The excitement among the people was intense. It was growing so that it was unwise for Christians to appear on the street. Even at the Legation we began to feel somewhat worried over what turn affairs might take. The populace of Teheran assembled in mobs near the palace of the Shah and the air was full of threats against his life. So it did not take him long to announce that the concession to the English was abolished in so far as it concerned tobacco for home use. But this did not appease the people in the least, nor did it cause the great mullah to remove the interdiction on the weed.

118

"Immediately the Shah summoned the great mullah and commanded him to appear in the mosque the next morning smoking his kalian, as a sign that the tobacco of Persia was no longer unclean. To this the mullah replied that Allah alone ruled over him and he would do nothing of the sort. The Shah ordered the high priest into exile.

"In that country when a famous man is banished he is ushered out with great ceremony and many camels. The usual preparations were made for the high priest, but when his caravan was ready to start the irate people refused to let the champion of their rights depart one step. All Teheran was in a tumult, and the leaders of the revolt made their way at once to the Shah's palace, forced the gates and demanded to see the Shah, this was refused and the outer guard was ordered to fire on the crowd. The guard, however, simply turned their guns the other way.

"Then the Islamites rushed toward the penetralia of the palace, where the Shah was hidden, surrounded by the picked body known as the Sholams of the Guard, men whose only devotion is to the person of the monarch.

" 'Bring out the Shah; we want to kill him,' shouted the people.

"Then the Sholams fired, wounding hundreds and killing a dozen of the green-turbaned men—lineal descendants of the Prophet.

"It was here that the rage of the defeated populace reached its height. Thousands of wild-eyed fanatics ran through the town, crying for the priests to authorize the 'jehad,' which means the massacre of all Christians.

"You may imagine the feelings of those in the eight foreign legations in Teheran. Thousands of miles from civilization, with the protective power of the Persian authorities completely collapsed, there would be but one possible end for all of us should the jehad be proclaimed.

"It was then that the American Minister, Truxtun Beale, came to the front. There were about a thousand Christian foreigners at the capital — Englishmen, Americans, Frenchmen, Belgians, Germans and others—many of them adventurous young men who had come out to seek their fortunes, or to fill positions in the telegraph service or with various commercial companies. As the situation grew more serious the house of the American Minister became the center of our planning, owing to the determined spirit and personal magnetism of Beale, who possesses the peculiar qualities of a born leader.

119

"Finally it began to look as if our goose was going to be cooked to a turn. A formal meeting of the eight foreign Ministers was held at one of the Legations, and Beale announced that for one he proposed to make it as interesting as he could for those who might attack the Legation, and that he intended to make his own life cost the Persians as many as possible.

"Four of the Ministers stood out from any scheme for a defensive alliance, but the remaining three agreed to band their forces together and fight to the last under the leadership of Truxtun Beale. To the disgust of all the English residents, their Minister seemed disinclined to make any resistance, and they flocked to the standard of Beale.

"Beale, however, succeeded in arranging that everybody who had fight in him should rendezvous at the British Legation, which was the most substantial of the eight, and that the women and children should be brought thither. He went about making arrangements for barricading the doors and windows. He laid in provisions, and all the arms and ammunition to be procured were placed there by the determined foreigners who had so much faith in Beale. He, remembering drift mining in California and the siege of Lucknow and how the scarcity of water undid the besieged, made connections with water tanks about the house in such manner as would supply enough water to last a long while. In a short time we were prepared to assemble at the first cry of 'Jehad' and sell our lives as dearly as possible.

"Well, it turned out that we didn't have to fight. The Shah, in fear of his own life, abolished all the rest of the tobacco concession, and immediately the Persian fell back under the influence of his beloved kalian. But if things had taken another direction history would have had another bloody chapter, and I know that the American Minister, Truxtun Beale, would have played a part in it of which his country would have been proud."

As the time neared for his return to the United States the Minister wished to take advantage of the opportunity of bringing back from Persia some things of scientific value. He realized that American stock breeders would profit from the importation of selected strains of livestock, such as a famous breed of Persian sheep. "I could not help noticing," he wrote, "the general similarity of physical and climatic conditions between Persia and California. When I heard of the merits of the fat-tailed sheep of Southern Persia I was satisfied they would adapt themselves perfectly to California conditions." Obtaining specimens of the breed involved an arduous 1,000-mile journey on horseback through desert country. He left Teheran and rode across the country to Ispahan, then to Persepolis, and on to the Persian Gulf. "I had no trouble," he reported, "in getting the twenty-five sheep I wanted, and by good luck found a tramp steamer on the point of leaving the Persian Gulf for England. I feel well repaid by knowing that this useful Persian strain is now established in California for all time."

Persepolis aroused his archaeological interest, and he saw an opportunity of bringing back to the United States some unique scientific material from the ancient ruins. The city of Persepolis, known in ancient times as "the glory of the East," had flourished under the Persian monarchs Darius and Xerxes before it was captured and sacked by Alexander the Great, and its imposing ruins still remained as reminders of the ancient past. Here were bas-reliefs and inscriptions of immense historical value, and Mr. Beale realized that it would be an important service to archaeology to bring them to the attention of the Western world. Working at the site was a British archaeologist making moulds of the inscriptions for the first time. Mr. Beale had the Shah's permission to take the stone originals, but he found them too cumbersome for transportation, and compromised for a series of *papier maché* moulds. These he had loaded on camels and taken to the Persian Gulf for shipment to the United States, where he presented them to the Smithsonian Institution. They were accorded considerable prominence at the time, as the first cuneiform inscriptions to reach the Western world.

The following year his work in Persia was recognized by an appointment to another diplomatic post, as Envoy Extraordinary and Minister Plenipotentiary to Greece. The court of the King of the Hellenes was a congenial assignment, and he enjoyed the country and the people, as well as taking great interest in the relics of the ancient world. His duties as Minister were increased by the current Chicago Exposition, and he facilitated Greek participation in this event. In 1892 his appointment was enlarged to include Rumania and Serbia, so that he served as Minister simultaneously to all three countries. Among other activities, he organized the American Diplomatic Aid in Europe, an organization which gave assistance to the town of Zante, destroyed by earthquake in 1893.

Of all countries there was none of greater archaeological interest than Greece, and the Minister saw an opportunity to supplement his official duties by procuring further antiquities. Only a few years before Heinrich Schliemann, "a shop-assistant who had read Homer," had startled the learned world with his sensational discovery of the site of ancient Troy in Asia Minor. Dr. Schliemann's excavations were made in the 1870's and again in 1889-90, just before his death. Mr. Beale's predecessor at the Greek court, A. Louden Snowden of Philadelphia, had besieged the widow of the great archaeologist for a share of the Trojan relics to be sent to the United States. She consented to give what remained after the Athens and Berlin museums had taken their pick. Dr. Snowden was then retiring from his post as Minister, and after his departure a forwarding agent went to Madam Schliemann to get what was described as "a box of things belonging to Dr. Snowden." At this point the lady consented to discuss the disposition of the relics with the new American Minister, Truxtun Beale. He succeeded in persuading her that the Trojan antiquities should go to the capital of the United States rather than to Philadelphia, and she agreed to give them to the Smithsonian Institution. As a kind of consolation prize, she said, "To Dr. Snowden I will give Dr. Schliemann's gold-headed cane." As soon as the matter was settled, the Minister got on his horse and rode down to the Piraeus, where he changed the shipping labels on the boxes.

The relics duly arrived in Washington, and were placed on exhibition at the Smithsonian. Their importance may be gauged from the fact that they are the only Trojan antiquities in the United States. The Minister was duly thanked by S. P. Langley, Secretary of the Smithsonian:

"Sir: I have been much gratified to learn, through the Department of State, of the gift from Madam Schliemann of a case containing a collection of antiquities discovered on the site of ancient Troy by Dr. Schliemann. This is not the first time that the Smithsonian Institution has had the pleasure of thanking you for your friendly and patriotic interest in behalf of the National Collections, and I wish to convey to you my assurances of very sincere appreciation of what you have done."

Truxtun Beale now decided to retire from the diplomatic service, in order to give more attention to his personal affairs, and on February 28, 1893 he cabled his father in Washington to tender his resignation to President Harrison. He had fulfilled his duties successfully, and had no desire for extended foreign service. Moreover, his father's health was failing, and he felt he was needed at home. Two months after his resignation his father died, and Truxtun Beale inherited Decatur House.

On April 30, 1894, he married Harriet S. Blaine, youngest daughter of James G. Blaine, whom Cleveland had narrowly defeated for the Presidency. The marriage was not a happy one. Their only child was born in 1896, and in opposition to his wishes was named Walker Blaine Beale. He requested a divorce, which was obtained the same year. Some time later he became reconciled to the little boy, and for the child's sake made an offer of remarriage, which never materialized.

In the meantime his travels carried him to a remote and inaccessible part of Asia, and he was the first American to cross the mountains between Siberia and Chinese Turkestan, a country penetrated thirty-two years later by the Roosevelt Expedition. His route he described in a letter from Vienna in 1896:

"I went into countries that few travellers have ever reached. I went to Central Asia and in Russian Turkestan I bought a little caravan of six horses, and crossed the Thian Shan range of mountains into Chinese Turkestan. Then after a week's hard riding I reached Kashgar in China. From there I struck north again, crossed the mountains by another pass, and got into Siberia. After crossing a portion of that country I reached the Trans-Siberian railroad, and by it came to Moscow and here. For many days travelling through the frontiers of China, I lived among the Kirghiz nomads in their tents."

He returned not to Washington but to California, preferring to live in the West after his unfortunate marriage. During the next few years he was concerned mainly with the administration of his business affairs. A graphic picture of how he appeared to the public eye is contained in the following description from the Chicago *Times Herald,* Nov. 4, 1899:

"Washington was his home until a few years ago. He now lives in San Francisco, where he superintends his vast sheep and cattle ranches, wheat farms and vineyards. He is also one of the richest and biggest wool merchants in the world, and ranks as such on two continents. While a resident of Washington he was looked upon as a dilettante member of the swell set. He was languid and never exterted himself to even make an impress in a social way, though belonging to the local aristocracy, which views with mingled contempt, amusement and tolerance the passing throng of statesmen, diplomats, officials and politicians, and the birth and death of administrations. On his removal to San Francisco he became a man of affairs, and was a big background figure in the fight for United States Senator last winter. He is likely to turn up at any time as Senator from California."

With a new maturity of outlook, he became increasingly concerned with the drift of national policy during these critical years. The country was now going through a period which the historian Beard has described as "the breach with historic continentalism." Beginning with the war with Spain in 1898, the destiny of the nation was conceived in worldwide terms, rather than on a continental scale, and the United States began plunging into world-power politics. Grasping immediately the tremendous implications of this, and with his firsthand knowledge of international affairs, Truxtun Beale was one of the first Americans of his generation to take up the study of the nation's role in the world politics of the future. During his residence in California he was the author of a series of pioneering analyses of America's new "place in the sun."

His first article, published in 1897, was largely a travel account of some of his experiences in Siberia, where he had visited some of the Russian prison camps and was favorably impressed with the humane treatment of the prisoners, contrary to the prevailing opinion. The article, entitled "Russian Humanity," was widely discussed, and his views did not fail to be quoted in Russian newspapers. An American reviewer of this article the same year made the following comment, which deserves to be preserved: "It is a real delight to hear from so reliable and observing a source that the Government of the foreign country which is perhaps the most friendly to the United States of all the nations of the world, is humane, rather than cruel."

His remarkable foresight was evident in a full-dress discussion of the comparative future strength of nations, published in the *Forum*, the following year. The title, "Our Interest in the Next Congress of the Powers," reflected his broad-scale but practical approach to the problems of American foreign policy. Again discussing the subject of Russia, this time in terms of her potential strength, he was one of the first to warn Americans of the latent danger in this quarter. Emphasizing the immense resources and increasing industrial progress of that country, he said: "While the Anglo-Saxon race is today the dominant race of the world, those who have seen the immense material development of Russia must admit that at the end of the next quarter century the relative power and influence of the Anglo-Saxon race will be much diminished." At the same time he stressed the need for continued development of international law.

Again anticipating vividly the course of global strategy for the United States, he published an article in the *North American Review* the same year on the "Strategical Value of the Philippines." His discussion of the military importance of the islands for the defence of the Pacific sounded a prophetic note, and created reverberations in European military journals. His estimate of the situation was confirmed some forty years later when war came to the Pacific.

His copious output of papers also encompassed political and economic aspects of global strategy. A much discussed problem at the time was whether the white race could ever succeed in permanent colonization of the tropics, and in the *Forum* of 1899 he summarized the advances in scientific knowledge that would make this goal possible. The importance of international trade in global politics was also the theme of his articles. For the International Commercial Congress in Philadelphia the same year he contributed a paper on "The Trade of Central Asia," as a key influence in the history of that area. Returning to the Russian problem, he contributed again to the *Forum* a warning concerning "Russia's Lien on Persia," in which he outlined some of the vital dangers that might arise from this source.

A more informal and amusing comment upon conditions in Central Asia was made by Mr. Beale when he was queried in a newspaper interview in 1901 concerning the subject of robbers and brigandage. Even here there was cause to refer to the efficiency of the Russians in the conquest of neighboring peoples. He said:

"The Russians have done wonders to make life and property secure in all parts of Central Asia, which they have recently conquered. Occasionally, murders and robberies are committed, but these are unusual. They content themselves with sneaking up on you from behind, when you are traveling in your sleigh, and cutting down your baggage and looting it. In fact, even in countries like Chinese Turkestan, which are outside the pale of Russian influence, one is comparatively safe. I have traveled with perfect safety for weeks among the Kirghiz, who in Spencer's *Sociology* are described as being a very fierce race. I have gone into their tents, lain down, and rested night or day. They might have harmed me, for they must have known that a traveler has large sums of money on his person. During my stay among these people not an article of mine was stolen. In fact, even when I performed my daily ablutions, I found it difficult to keep the men and women out of my tent, as they seemed fearful lest I might steal something which belonged to them."

Among his writings during this period, perhaps Mr. Beale's most widely discussed one was another *Forum* piece entitled "The Education of the Millionaire." In reply to Thomas Nelson Page, who had severely criticized the habits of the social circle at Newport, Mr. Beale undertook to defend these social leaders against such charges as arrogance and playing croquet on Sunday. But he found the opportunity irresistible to add some acid comments of his own. His chief target was "spendthrift expenditure" among the millionaire class: "While our *nouveaux riches* do not all consider it necessary to drink themselves to death on gin, in order properly to distribute their wealth, like the one mentioned by Leslie Stephen, nevertheless, nearly all of them spend it in many ways hardly more useful to themselves and society." The article created a passing furor among his friends.

Truxtun Beale

A little episode reflecting the more intimate and humorous side of his nature found its way into a newspaper item in 1902:

"He was continually flitting from his ranch in Kern County, the Tejon, to San Francisco, and when in town he lived at the Pacific Union Club. He would drift into the club in the afternoon, in negligé attire—flannel shirt, no waistcoat, and an old tweed shooting jacket. How he did shock the sensibilities of shoddy commercialism, spick and span in fine linen and broadcloth! One of them — a certain red-polled parrakeet — grew so distressed brooding over Beale's costume that he actually chattered a complaint to the committee. Thereafter Beale appeared, morning, noon and night, in a silk-lined frock coat, white four-in-hand, patent leathers and lavender kids. He declined to remove his gloves even when at the table, and studiously refused each proffered hand, because, so he averred, the members were such a dowdy lot. At the end of a week the directors besought him to cry quits, and next morning Beale appeared in his old tweeds, but radiant."

There was an unusually sensitive and sympathetic side to his nature, which made him invariably responsive to those in distress, even strangers. About this time a small personal incident occurred which elicited an unexpected tribute years later. A man, hurrying from New York to the bedside of his sick father in California, encountered Truxtun Beale on a transcontinental train. He afterwards wrote:

"I had known of Mr. Beale but had never met him. He strolled into the club car the evening we left Chicago, and for some reason came over and spoke to me. Perhaps he may have sensed my anxiety. From that moment he was attentive, his personality and optimism most comforting. We talked of many things, including a hurried voyage he once made to New York from Southampton when his father was seriously ill. I left the train at Sacramento at six in the morning, a rather early hour for travelers to be up and about; nevertheless Mr. Beale was in the vestibule to say goodbye. I never saw Mr. Beale again, but the sincerity and kindliness of the man was fixed in my memory."

However, there was a sterner side to his nature, for life in California at the beginning of the century still retained much of the rugged forthrightness of its earlier years, when the word "liar" was usually followed by an inquest. One of the less savory aspects of this period was a type of sensational journalism, irresponsibly focussed on prominent persons. Among the occupational hazards of the journalist was occasional assault and battery at the hands of the aggrieved victim or his friends, this being the only possible means of redress, common enough at the time. Eventually Truxtun Beale joined the ranks of those who believed in direct measures, for he became incensed over an article about some of his friends and paid a visit to the editor. Accounts of the incident were varied and inconclusive. It seems that he was accompanied by a quick-tempered companion, and that there was a considerable *melée*, during which the editor received a bullet wound in the leg. Who fired the shot was never ascertained. The entire episode created a short-term sensation.

While he lived in California, Mr. Beale frequently came to Washington to visit his mother at Decatur House, where she lived until her death. By the turn of the century the original "treeless commons" in front of Decatur House had evolved into a city park, a typical example of the open square characteristic of American cities. The rectangle covering two city blocks had been laid out with winding walks leading up to the Jackson monument, and was planted with a diversity of trees and shrubbery, partly formal after the Continental fashion in gardens, but with elements of English naturalism as well. In 1891 the Square had acquired a statue of its namesake, La Fayette, an imposing work designed by the French sculptors Falguiere and Mercie, and erected in the southeast corner of the park. France donated a companion piece in honor of Rochambeau, which was unveiled in 1902 in the southwest corner. A few years later two other European military leaders who took part in the American Revolution were honored with memorials at the other corners of the park, Kosciusko and Von Steuben. The development of La Fayette Square was complete.

A renovation of the White House was undertaken in 1902 by the New York architectural firm of McKim, Meade and White, at the behest of the new President who had succeeded the assassinated McKinley, Theodore Roosevelt. The chandeliers in the East Room were removed and sent over to the Capitol, to be replaced by others of later design. More changes were made to modernize the Executive Mansion. The old furnishings had been similarly ravaged just twenty years before, under the regime of Chester A. Arthur, when twenty-four wagonloads of furniture and other household articles, including rat-traps, were sold at public auction. During the 1902 renovation, President Roosevelt lived in another house on La Fayette Square, at 736 Jackson Place, a mid-nineteenth century structure still standing.

The following year Decatur House welcomed a bride. On April 23, 1903, Truxtun Beale was married in New York to Marie Chase Oge, daughter of Mr. and Mrs. William L. Oge, of San Rafael, California. Washington society greeted the couple with receptions and entertainments, and after they came to live permanently in Washington Decatur House entered upon a new period of social activity. When finally reopened, the house again became a popular rendezvous for the social and political figures of Washington.

At the time of his marriage, Truxtun Beale was forty-seven years of age, and a popular personage in both California and Washington. In appearance he was short and stocky, with blue eyes and blond hair, not good looking, but with a charming smile. He walked with something of a rolling gait, a sailor's inheritance, his friends said. In temperament he was a blend of contrasting qualities, energetic but sensitive, with a high temper but quick to forget, and responsive to appeals for help. He had a quick and able mind, fortified by wide reading, particularly in political science and economics. Athletically inclined, he was a skillful boxer and liked outdoor diversions, except horseback riding. His interests were more nautical, and he would canoe anywhere, in San Francisco Bay, at Newport, on the Seine, the Thames or the Potomac. In personal contacts he was distinguished by kindliness and humor, but like Livingston he was not a good judge of men.

He enjoyed spending part of each year at the Tejon Rancho, which a manager operated in his absence. He and his wife traveled often in Europe as well. But as the years passed they found their interests centered more and more in Washington, and in the pleasant circle of life at Decatur House. This shift of interest, combined with the difficulties of administering a large estate from a distance, culminated with the sale of the Tejon properties in 1912, after which the Beales resided wholly at Decatur House. During the final two years before the sale of the Tejon Mr. Beale served as Regent of the University of California.

As the twentieth century moved onward, Mr. Beale became increasingly aware of a trend or drift of national policy that eventually induced him once again to publish his own timely views. Again he was one of the first of his generation in America to call attention to a fresh aspect of contemporary developments, this time in the domestic rather than the international field. He was qualified for this by more than twenty years of practical experience in large-scale financial operations involving the actual production of wealth in terms of what people eat and wear and use. In the field of American business enterprise he perceived a growing menace, small at first but rapidly becoming more formidable, and set about to draw public attention to it.

Others have since become alarmed at the increasing encroachment of power by the state, and have done much to mobilize public opinion against it, but considerable credit must be given to those farsighted men who first realized the potential menace of state control as a factor in American life. As the best line of attack then available, Mr. Beale utilized the work of Herbert Spencer, whose book *The Man Versus the State* was an effective warning against this very trend. In 1915 Mr. Beale prepared and edited a symposium on the same subjected, entitled *The State Versus the Man.*

The book consisted of Spencer's essays, to which Mr. Beale added a carefully collected group of critical and interpretive comments by contemporary leaders: William Howard Taft, Charles W. Eliot, Elihu Root, Henry Cabot Lodge, David Jayne Hill, Nicholas Murray Butler, Augustus P. Gardner, E. H. Gary and Harlan F. Stone, an extraordinary galaxy of prominent Americans. A foreword to the book declared: "It is due to the interest and energy of Mr. Truxtun Beale that these essays of Herbert Spencer, with comments by eminent Americans, have been gathered together into a book. Mr. Beale has been a student and a disciple of Spencer ever since he became acquainted with his work; he has, indeed, been a sort of lay exponent of the

Spencerian philosophy in America. . . . Mr. Beale traveled about the country enlisting the aid of a few of those leaders of thought in America who know the tremendous value of Spencer's work in our social system; and he succeeded in inducing these men to write critical and interpretive comments on the essays, as they appear in the light of what they can teach us in relation to the problems that are perplexing America today."

In Mr. Beale's contribution to the symposium, entitled "The State Versus the Man in America," he took a position that might be described as measured and enlightened conservatism. He discerned the need for a new force in American politics, a conservative party committed to "progress with resistance," that is to say, resistance to undesirable trends. Foremost among these tendencies, he pointed out, was the mushrooming of bureaucratic agencies, with the attendant mischiefs of overlegislation and overadministration; the result he summarized as "the blight of officialism." Existing parties, he declared, vied with each other in advocating state agencies or state controls, yet in actual practice officialism was slow, expensive, unadaptive and unprogressive in the long run. He was too careful a thinker, however, to endorse the "administrative nihilism" of Spencer, but ably indicated there was a middle ground between this extreme and the towering menace of the total state. It may be fairly said that his quest for a middle ground on this issue foreshadowed the major tradition of subsequent American thought.

In the course of Mr. Beale's life he made many gifts for civic and educational projects. In 1900 he presented the Beale Memorial Library to the city of Bakersfield, California, in memory of his father, and subsequently endowed a university expansion program in the same city, including a university park and an outdoor Greek theatre. The idea of transplanting the New England "town meeting" system to Washington suburban communities appealed to him as a civic project, and in 1916 he presented a town hall building to the Potomac District of Montgomery County, for community use. His objective was to encourage a more active interest in community affairs, and he stipulated that every gathering in the hall should include a discussion of local problems. In Annapolis, Maryland, he gave a 32-acre public park on Spa Creek, named after his great grandfather, Commodore Truxtun. He also established a series of university prizes totaling $10,000 as a memorial to his son, Walker Blaine Beale, who was killed in action in France in the closing days of the first World War.

Truxtun Beale died at his country home, near Annapolis, June 2, 1936. A diplomat, writer, lawyer, rancher, explorer, and leader of Washington society, he had had one of the most diversified careers of his generation, and had excelled in many fields. Born in a turbulent frontier settlement, he had witnessed in the course of his life the development of modern America. A striking and colorful personality, rich, brilliant and eccentric, he was a man "made for wide spaces, physical and mental." He gave to many causes, helping to support hospitals and aiding the blind. Active to the end, he made long canoe trips in the closing months of his life, before his death at the age of eighty years. He was buried at historic Bruton Parish Church in Williamsburg, Virginia, where his ancestors had worshipped.

ST. JOHN'S CHURCH, LAFAYETTE SQUARE, BUILT BY LATROBE.
FROM A WATER COLOR BY LATROBE IN 1818 SHOWING WHITE HOUSE AT RIGHT
(Property of St. John's Church)

CHAPTER XII

DECATUR HOUSE TODAY

HENRY ADAMS describes in his autobiography how he often stood at the window of his Washington home, looking out over La Fayette Square and musing over the great men and women of the past whose lives were centered there. No doubt many others have done the same before and since. Here was the common meeting ground of so many historical personages that it could be called, perhaps, the center of the political history of the nation. More than any other single spot in America this little plot of ground was still animate with the past, still quietly redolent of bygone days, still preserving the faint echo of the footsteps of those who led the country to greatness. The past is still mirrored in the historic residences that surround it, where so many of these people lived or visited. American life owes much to La Fayette Square.

In the Square today much remains and much is gone. Across from the White House, St. John's is one of the city's principal churches, though altered considerably over the years. At one corner of the Square the residence of the brother of Dolly Madison, which later became that of Dolly Madison, has been a clubhouse, in conjunction with the Benjamin Ogle Tayloe place, known during the Hanna occupancy as "the Little White House." Gone is the "elegant" mansion of Commodore John Rodgers, where Seward was felled by the assassin's knife, and afterwards the home of the "plumed knight," James G. Blaine. Also among the casualties of time are the Corcoran house, originally the house given by the nation to Daniel Webster, and the double structure designed by Richardson for Henry Adams and John Hay. Just off the Square the Blair House, rich in historical associations, is now owned by the Government and used as an official residence for distinguished guests. In the center of the Square Andrew Jackson still rears his carrousel steed and doffs his hat in perpetual salute to nothing in particular. Presiding over the Square, the

133

Georgian mansion of the Chief Executive retains from its past only its walls.

Like a prim dowager, Decatur House serenely overlooks the park that grew up in its front yard, preserving unchanged its original sturdy simplicity. During more than 130 years of intimate connection with the main stream of American history Decatur House has been the inner sanctum of La Fayette Square. Few houses have witnessed such a panorama of events. Here the dying Decatur suffered out his last hours. Here foreign Ministers represented the power and policies of other nations. Henry Clay struggled here for the Good Neighbor Policy and the Presidency, attaining one but not the other. The "gorgeous hussy" Peggy Eaton quarrelled here with the wife of the Chief of Staff, and the astute Van Buren moved on to the White House and subsequent defeat. In this house the great jurist Livingston had averted the first secession threat by South Carolina. The gaudy Gadsby lived here, the unimpeachable Dallas, and the benevolent Appleton. Two leaders of the Confederate cause, Cobb and Benjamin, walked these floors as they reached the most momentous decision of their lives, and renounced their country. After the interim of the Civil War years, a General and President, Ulysses S. Grant, came here for friendship and counsel from General Beale, himself one of the architects of the American West, a "pioneer in the path of empire." Through the tumultuous period that followed, Truxtun Beale preserved the historic role of Decatur House in the life of Washington. Residents of Decatur House have occupied the Presidency and Vice Presidency; they have been Cabinet members, military leaders, Congressmen; they have been foreign diplomats and American envoys to other nations; the roster includes Confederate statesmen, a jurist and an inn-keeper. By all of them Decatur House was valued, and perhaps beloved.

As the last private owner of Decatur House, I Marie Beale, have inherited the responsibility of bringing this historic career to a graceful close. The passing years have brought a new era in the life of La Fayette Square, now a museum-piece, hallowed by association with the great figures and events of the past. Decatur House, too, has undergone a similar transformation. As it had been the first private residence on La Fayette Square, so now it has become the last and the Beale family have been its longest

134

occupants. Thus its lifetime bracketed an epoch from beginning to end. Like La Fayette Square, Decatur House belongs to history.

In recent years a concerted effort has been made, in England, France, Italy and elsewhere, to protect and preserve historic homes and buildings. Special agencies have been created to prevent the destruction of these irreplaceable treasures, and to preserve them for future generations. In the United States, as well, we can scarcely escape the realization that a nation should preserve its memorials of the past as an obligation to the future. Efforts in this direction heretofore have been scattered and piecemeal. Recently a private organization has been formed in the United States to undertake a concerted national program toward this end, The National Trust for Historic Preservation. Through this organization, I have bequeathed Decatur House to future generations as a national monument.

This decision was the outgrowth of my fifty years of association with Decatur House, in which time I, its last and longest resident, have shaped my efforts toward this ultimate end. My half-century with Decatur House began in 1903, upon my marriage to Truxtun Beale.

During the course of my childhood in the old mission town of San Rafael, California, I was steeped in the Spanish atmosphere and traditions from the early Dons who originally settled there, and acquired a lifelong affection for the culture of Spanish America. This was the fortunate origin, also, of a deep historical interest and a corresponding appreciation of the necessity of preserving historical sites and mementoes. My own family had been connected in various ways with the development of the country; a great-grandfather Philander Chase, bishop of the Anglican Episcopal Church, was sent out from New England to establish the church in what was then the West, the States of Ohio and Illinois, and also founded Kenyon College. Another ancestor was Salmon P. Chase, one-time Secretary of the Treasury and later Chief Justice of the United States. I came as a young bride to Decatur House, which thereafter remained the center of my long and fairly active life.

In addition to the Washington residence, we spent many winters on that vast domain, the Tejon Ranchos in California, that

General Beale had acquired. It was still conducted in the Spanish fashion, employing many Mexican and Indian *vaqueros,* who tended the cattle and sheep. The *mayor domo* of the place was a worthy who bore the name of Jésus Lopez, and the owner was called the "patron." Many of the people on the place came to me, the *patrona,* with their personal problems, as their forebears had in the early Spanish days, and I advised them in their own tongue, for I had as a companion a young woman descended from one of the great Spanish rancheros of California who gave me constant instruction during our daily rides and drives over the open country and into the circling mountains. For a period of years we alternated in residence between Decatur House and this semi-baronial western domain.

In Washington, Decatur House continued to uphold its tradition as a center of political and social life, but after the 1920's it became the last remaining representative of the historic hospitality of the Square. As in its first days, guests now came to only two places in La Fayette Square—the President's Mansion and Decatur House—which somehow symbolized the completion of a long cycle. Any incongruous modernization of the old place had been avoided, and the candle-lighted drawing rooms, with their wealth of mementoes, provided an effective setting for social gatherings. I have realized, as well as do my guests, that all this represented the end of an era.

The Spanish background of the early settlement of America has exerted a constant attraction for me, and led to a number of visits to Latin America. In 1931 I returned from a visit to Ambassador and Mrs. Robert Woods Bliss in Buenos Aires by a then-novel flight across the Andes mountains, and continued up the west coast of South America. I studied the Inca remains in Peru and the Mayan cities of Yucatan, and from my experiences and observations I wrote a book entitled *Flight Into America's Past,* which was published in 1933. My archaeological interests culminated in establishing, with Dr. Alexander Kidder and with the help of Mr. Bliss, the Institute of Andean Research, which has accomplished notable progress in the field of American archaeology. Among other projects, it provided technical backing for the epochal work of Julio C. Tello, a brilliant Peruvian scientist of

CANDLE LIGHTING AT DECATUR HOUSE

ENTRANCE HALL OF DECATUR HOUSE

End of Second Floor Drawing Room
of Decatur House

IMPERIAL RUSSIAN EMBASSY CARRIAGE, WITH COSSACK FOOTMAN, AWAITING
MARY BEALE BAHKMÉTEFF, THE AMBASSADRESS AND DAUGHTER
OF EDWARD F. BEALE, IN FRONT OF DECATUR HOUSE

pure Indian blood, who made many contributions to the study of pre-Colombian cultures and under whose spell I had fallen on my first vist to Peru.

In furtherance of the Good Neighbor Policy associated with Henry Clay at the time of his residence in Decatur House, and which coincided with my own inclinations, I welcomed several opportunities for practical manifestations of friendship toward Latin American nations. On the occasion of another trip, after the outbreak of the second World War, I discovered that the National Library of Ecuador had no representation of books from the United States, and upon my return presented to the library a new section of volumes to remedy this lack. Similarly, upon learning that fire had ravaged the collection of the National Library at Lima, Peru, I contributed towards its restoration, in recognition of which the Peruvian Government in 1947 conferred upon me the order of "El Sol del Peru."

During my years of residency the furnishings and *objets d'art* at Decatur House have been retained largely intact, wherever possible. There have been two notable additions of works of art of the highest quality. One is a Greek head of Pentellic marble dating from the fourth century B.C. It was originally brought to Washington by the Imperial Russian Ambassador, George Bakhmétéff, who married General Beale's eldest daughter. In the course of a distinguished diplomatic career he had acquired the beautiful Greek fragment at Athens, from its original excavator, and jealously guarded it during his travels, carrying it under his arm as his wife carried her pet Pekingese. It is of the same era as the Lansdowne head at the Metropolitan Museum, New York, and bears a strong resemblance to a head of Scopas in the National Museum at Athens. Another important work of art brought to Decatur House is a Renaissance bronze, probably an Eve, and judged by experts at the Fogg Museum to be the product of a North Italian studio. Both these works have been frequently exhibited.

The war years were a period of heightened activity at Decatur House, which served for a number of wartime activities. Many men and women of the armed services were entertained there on various occasions. At the special request of the State Department much additional entertaining was done on behalf of Latin American guests, because the house had long been associated with the Good Neighbor policy toward these nations, and in 1944 the Secretary of State, Cordell Hull, expressed the Department's appreciation of these endeavors. I also took an active part in war relief campaigns to help the Allied nations, particularly England, France, Italy and Greece. Attracted particularly to the Greek cause, since my late husband had been Minister to that country, I supervised campaigns for donations, arranged lectures and exhibits, and promoted other activities. For my services George II, King of the Hellenes, conferred upon me in 1946 the Gold Cross of the Order of Phoenix. I arranged for the donation of a "Truxtun Unit" ambulance to the British - American Ambulance Corps, and headed a benefit program for the aid fund of the Royal Air Force, which at that time was holding "the common frontier of democracy." I also participated in French and Italian war relief work.

The aftermath of the war opened another avenue of historical and cultural interest. Going to Venice in 1946, I found a considerable degree of anxiety prevailing in regard to the progressive deterioration of some of the city's finest buildings. The waters of the Venetian canals, over a period of centuries, threatened with erosion the ancient foundations, many of them dating from the heydey of the Venetian Republic, 600 years ago, and some of them older. Seriously threatened was the most imposing building in the city, Saint Mark's Basilica, one of the best known churches in the world. This magnificent example of Byzantine art, resting partly on wooden piles in the Venetian estuary, had not suffered directly from wartime damage like many other buildings, but indirectly through the cessation of repairs and preservative measures during the war years. The great structure was imperilled by crumbling walls, and its ancient mosaics were falling away. "The preservation of San Marco," said the art critic Berenson, "is more important than that of any monument damaged by the war."

The curator of the Basilica, the renowned Marangoni, appealed to me for assistance in securing funds for this purpose in America. Upon my return to the United States I organized a group of

DOORWAY OF DECATUR HOUSE AFTER RESTORATION, 1944
(Photo by T. T. Waterman)

Slave Quarters at Decatur House.
From a water color by V. E. Soderberg, June 1939,
hanging at the top of stairway in Decatur House

eminent Americans to help save for posterity this precious monument of Western civilization. "Pro San Marco, Inc." was promptly formed, with John Nicholas Brown as Chairman, and Mrs. Duncan Phillips and me as officers. Aid was enlisted from prominent art patrons, and by this means a substantial sum was raised and sent to Italy to make possible the needed repairs. In recognition of my work toward the restoration of Saint Mark's Basilica, I was made in 1952, on my annual visit, an honorary citizen of Venice in a ceremony at the Ducal Palace.

It was a golden afternoon of the 6th of September. We were ushered up the great staircases to the *Sala del Collegio,* where the magnificent Veronese and the Tintorettos looked down from the ceiling and walls. All the Commune authorities were there, headed by the *Sindaco,* or Mayor, Professor Angelo Spanio; the *Procuratoria,* or governing body for the Basilica of St. Marks, and the representatives of the Patriarch of Venice, who was ill, as well as other clergy.

The halls soon filled with citizens of Venice, my friends from all over Italy, and even some very dear ones who had come all the way from London.

When four o'clock came I was led to the stage and seated in the front line beside the *Sindaco.* This tall and very handsome man arose and read the resolution of the Commune conferring the honorary citizenship on me, from a beautifully illuminated parchment which he then presented to me. It read as follows:

By public resolution the city of Venice expressed its thanks, saying: "In 1948 she took the initiative of forming in the United States a committee of distinguished persons for the collecting of funds destined to the conservation of the Basilica of Saint Mark's. She distinguished herself in this matter, aside from her personal conspicuous contributions, by pursuing with constant enthusiasm the gathering of funds in the succeeding years. While Europe was still oppressed from the consequences of the war, the gesture of the American committee showed the solidarity of the United States with Italy, turning as it did to save spiritual values and the beauties of art in a form of high social significance. Mrs. Truxtun Beale, who inspired it with her exquisite comprehension, deserves the highest gratitude of the civic administration of Venice, as well as that of the committee of the Basilica."*

They also gave me a mass of pink roses tied with red ribbon, embroidered with the Lion of St. Mark's. They also gave me a small bronze copy of the Colleoni equestrian statue by Verocchio which stands in the Piazza of San Giovanni e Paolo. It is known the world over, along with the Donatello statue of Gattamelata in Padua.

Then, my knees knocking together, I had to rise and give thanks in Italian. One of my friends had composed a very flowery speech which I felt was not only beyond my powers to deliver, but not at all my style. He remonstrated that the Italians, very eloquent themselves and born orators, would expect something like that from me, but I contented myself by saying that I was profoundly moved to receive this parchment by virtue of which I became what I had already really been in my heart for some time— a citizen of Venice; that I had always had a great love for their— now *our*—city and nothing could give me greater pleasure than this demonstration of regard on the part of Venetians.

It was then the turn of the First *Procurator* of the Basilica, who was also a Deputy of the National Chamber and a renowned speaker. He recounted the history of Venice from earliest times, all without a single note. I was fascinated by his histrionic powers.

Their gift to me was a large mosaic copied from the original in the Basilica, of the head of St. Mark and executed by the Basilica's artist workmen. I thanked them for this touching souvenir, especially because it showed that the workmen had understood what I had always emphasized in giving contributions to Pro San Marco, Inc., namely, that all our monies should be used to pay labor. Our organization had realized that after a crisis such as the war, these artists would be the last to be employed and that they too, like the common workman who was building bridges, restoring railroads, motor-roads and housing, had families to feed and clothe.

---

* Translated from the illuminated parchment presented to me by the *Sindaco* and Commune of Venice at the ceremony. It now hangs in the library of Decatur House.

MARIE BEALE
FROM A PASTEL PORTRAIT BY YAGO

Everyone was then invited into the neighboring *Sala del Consiglio* where refreshments were served. Thus concluded one of the most memorable days of my life.

There was an amusing incident connected with the shipment home of these trophies. The bronze of the Colleoni had been already packed when we were told that permission must be had from the Customs to send it out of the country, it being classed as a work of art. It seems unbelievable but the clerk, when told that in the box was the copy of the statue, suspiciously observed, "How do I know that it is not the original!"

In the United States the preservation of historic buildings, fortunately, is not a matter of rescuing them from the deterioration of many centuries, as in Italy, but nevertheless they require attention and care. Decatur House is happily situated in that its sturdy structure needs no basic repair. I have pursued a policy in general of leaving it undisturbed, except in the case of two special alterations to increase its beauty and usefulness. Some mid-Victorian decorations that had been added to the doorway and front windows were removed in 1944, to regain the original severe purity of Latrobe's design. This restoration of the façade, executed by Thomas T. Waterman, received favorable notice in architectural circles as enhancing "a perfect gem of architecture." The only other significant change has been the addition of a new feature, the Truxtun-Decatur Naval Museum.

Washington acquired another museum for its residents when the Truxtun-Decatur Naval Museum was opened on May 12, 1950. It is situated in a building on H Street that was formerly the carriage house of the Decatur residence, now extensively remodeled and operated as a museum by the Naval Historical Foundation. Here historical mementoes of the American Navy are on public display, "to unfold dramatically and educationally the potent history of the country's maritime development." The building contains carefully planned exhibition rooms and other facilities serving its purpose. The Naval Historical Foundation was organized in 1926 as a repository for the "vanishing sources of our maritime history and traditions," and it is accumulating an ever-increasing store of documents, mementoes, pictures, weapons, uniforms, ship models and other relics.

When Fleet Admiral Ernest J. King, head of the Foundation, asked me if I did not have some space in the slave quarters or the stables where they could open a small museum, it seemed to me impossible. I kept my motor in the carriage house giving on H Street and thus was able to walk through the house to enter the motor in case of bad weather. And all sorts of things were stored, firewood, garden furniture, tools and, as always where there is plenty of space, much trash. I finally decided that it could be done and that I would use the space giving on the alley for my garage. We then drew up a lease giving the Foundation the use of the property opening on H Street in consideration of a dollar a year. This has enabled them to display in rotation the material of their large collection. Every three or four months they put on a new show and having already attracted over 100,000 visitors, they find their membership increasing. The cost of adapting the building was defrayed by public subscription and the museum is now open daily without charge.

For a long period the shadow of condemnation hung over Decatur House, when it was felt in some quarters that La Fayette Square should be "ringed" with white stone buildings of a public character, but the more recent trend toward urban decentralization has removed such pressure. In 1935 Congress passed the Historic Sites Act, declaring it to be a matter of national policy to preserve historic sites and buildings, and the Department of the Interior was directed to make a national survey of such places to determine their importance. Decatur House, of course, was included in this "Historic American Buildings Survey." As a result, Decatur House was designated a site of national historical importance, "as possessing exceptional historic and architectural interest and as being worthy of most careful preservation for the benefit of future generations."

NAME INDEX

NAME INDEX

A

Adams, Henry 115, 133
—John Quincy 16, 18, 21,
   23, 38, 45
—family 56
Africa 109
Albany, N. Y. 31, 38
Aleppo 44
Alexander I, Czar 17-8
Alexander the Great 121
Alexandria, Egypt 110
Alexandria, Va. 47-9
Alexandria Dancing Assembly 49
Alexandria Theatre 48
Algiers 9
Ammen, Daniel 109
Andes Mountains 136
Andrassy Jules 108
Annapolis, Md. 45, 131-2
Appleton, William 57
Appomattox, Va. 64
Arctic 82
Argus (brig) 5, 8
Arizona 107
Arlington Hotel 111
Arthur, Chester A. 112, 129
Ashland, Ky. 22
Asia Minor 44
Aspinwall, G. W. 83-4
Athens, Greece 122
Atlantic Ocean 109
Austria-Hungary 107-8, 116

B

Bacourt, Adolphe, chevalier de 51
Bagdad 44
Bainbridge, Joseph 5
—William 5, 8, 11-2
Bakersfield, Calif. 101, 131
Bakhmétéff, George 137
Baltimore, Md. 47, 53
Bancroft, George 21, 31
Barnum, Phineas T. 79
Barron, James 10-3
Barton, Cora 105-6
—Thomas P. 37

Bathurst, Lord 44
Beale, Miss 67, 137
—Edward Fitzgerald 55, 67-8,
   72-5, 114-5, 136
—Emily (Truxtun) 69-70,
   109-10, 112
—George 68-9
—Harriett (Blaine) 123
—Marie (Oge) 115, 129, 133-42
—Mary (Edwards) 79-81, 93-4,
   109-114, 128
—Thomas 68
—Truxtun 94-5, 106-7, 113-32,
   135
—Walker Blaine 123, 132
—family 68-9, 134-5
Beale Memorial Library 131
Benjamin, Judah P. 61-3
—Natalie (St. Martin) 61-4
Benton, Thomas Hart 43, 76, 78
Bering Strait 82
Berlin, Germany 122
Berlin, Md. 5
Berri, France 16
Bladensburg, Md. 11-2
Blaine, Harriett S.   *See* Beale, Harriett
   (Blaine)
—James G. 113, 123, 133
Blair House 64, 133
Bliss, Mildred (Barnes) 136
—Robert Woods, 136
Bloomingdale, D. C. 68, 75
Bodega Bay 71
Bolivar Simon 23
Bombay 110
Bonaparte, Jerome 4
Borie, Mr. 110
Bourbon, House of 16
Braddock, Edward 68
British West Indies 61
Brown, John 59
—John Nicholas 139
Bruton Parish Church 68, 132
Bryant, William Cullen 31
Buchanan, James 59-60
Buenos Aires 136
Burke, Edmund 42

145

146

N

Napoleon I 4
National Hotel 47
National Intelligencer 56-7
National Library of Ecuador 137
National Trust for Historic Preservation 135
Naval Historical Foundation 141-2
Nelson, Horatio, Viscount 7
Nevada 85
New Jersey 56
New Orleans, La. 39-40, 61
New York 2, 56, 105, 127
New York (ship) 5
Newport, R. I. 126, 129
Newport News, Va. 112
Niagara 2
Nordhoff, Charles 102
Norfolk, Va. 4, 48
Norris, Mr. 83
North American 80
North Pole 81-2

O

Oge, Marie Chase. *See* Beale, Marie (Oge)
—William L. 129
O'Neill, Margaret "Peggy". *See* Eaton, Margaret (O'Neill)
—William 24-5, 49
Oxford, England 44
Ozier, Judge 95

P

Pacific Ocean 92, 125
Page, Thomas Nelson 126
Panama 70, 76
Paredes, Mariano 77
Paris 62
Parkinson, Richard 47
Paullin, Charles O. 13
Penn, William 80
Pennsylvania 10, 53
Pennsylvania Avenue 15, 50, 52, 67
Pennsylvania Railroad 112
Perry, Oliver Hazard 5
Persepolis, Pa. 121
Persia 44, 115, 117-21
Persian Gulf 121
Peru 136-7
Petersburg, Va. 48
Philadelphia, Pa. 5, 48-9

Philadelphia (frigate) 4, 6-7, 12
Philippine Islands 125-6
Phillips, Duncan B. 139
Pierce, Edward 1
—Franklin K. 56
—family 1
Piraeus, Greece 122
Pitt, William 21, 56
Pogson, Mr. 113
Poletika, P. I. 17
Polk, James K. 35, 53, 55, 79
Porter, David 4
—David D. 88
Portugal 17, 109
Potomac River 2, 11, 49, 129
Powers, Jack 102
Preble, Edward 6-7
President (frigate) 9-10
President's House. *See* White House
President's Square. *See* Lafayette Square
Princeton University 38
Pro San Marco, Inc. 139-40

Q

Quincy, Josiah 42

R

Randolph, John of Roanoke 24, 30
Richard, Henry H. 133
Richmond, Va. 22, 48
Richmond (ship) 110
Riggs family 85
Rio de Janeiro 17
Rio Grande River 54
Rochambeau, Donatien Marie de Vimeur, comte de 128
Rocky Mountains 98
Rodgers, John 43, 115, 133
Rome, Italy 9
Romundo (Indian) 114
Roosevelt, Theodore 123, 128-9
Root, Elihu 130
Rube, Capt. 83
Rugby, England 44
Rumsey, James 49
Rumania 115, 121
Russia 17-21, 44, 54-5, 124-6

S

Sacramento, Calif. 55, 76
St. John's Episcopal Church 1-2, 59, 67, 133

W

Washington, George 47-9, 68
Washington, D. C. 11, 47, 53, 111
Waterman, Thomas Tileston 141
Webster, Daniel 30, 43, 133
—family 56
Weehawken, N. J. 12
Wellington Channel 82
What Cheer House 106
White House 1-2, 21, 25, 29, 49,
    52, 54, 68, 70, 128-9, 134, 136
Wheeler, Mr. 8
Williamsburg, Va. 132
Winchester, Va. 48
Wise, John 47
Wood, Frank F. 112

Wool, John Ellis 90-1
Wythe, George 22

X

Xerxes, 121

Y

York, Pa. 48
York County, Va. 68-9
Yucatan 136

Z

Zante, Greece 122
Zuni 91

151

BIBLIOGRAPHY

Adams, Henry, *History of the United States of America*, 1889-91.

——, *The Education of Henry Adams*, 1918.

Adams, John Quincy, *Writings of John Quincy Adams*, ed. by W. C. Ford, 1913-17.

Adams, John Quincy, *Memoirs, comprising portions of his Diary from 1795-1848*, ed. by Charles Francis Adams, 1874-77.

Alexander, Holmes, *The American Talleyrand*, 1935.

Allen, G. W., *Our Navy and the Barbary Corsairs*, 1905.

——, *Our Naval War with France*, 1909.

Bancroft, George, *Martin Van Buren*, 1889.

Bassett, John S., *Life of Andrew Jackson*, 1931.

Beale, Marie, *Flight Into America's Past*, 1933.

Beale, Truxtun, (ed.) *The State Versus the Man*, 1915.

Beard, Charles A., *Economic Origins of Jeffersonian Democracy*, 1915.

Bemis, Samuel F., (ed.) *The American Secretaries of State and Their Diplomacy*, 1927-29.

Bemis, Samuel F., *A Diplomatic History of the United States*, 1942.

Benton, Thomas Hart, *Thirty Years' View*, 1854-56.

Binkley, Wilfred E., *American Political Parties*, 1943.

Blair, Gist, "Lafayette Square", in *Records of the Columbia Historical Society*, vol. 28 (1926), pp. 133-73.

Bonsal, Stephen, *Edward Fitzgerald Beale, A Pioneer in the Path of Empire*, 1912.

Bruce, W. C., *John Randolph of Roanoke*, 1922.

Bryan, Wilhelmus B., *A History of the National Capital*, 1916.

Caemmerer, H. P., *A Manual on the Origin and Development of Washington*, 1939.

——, *Washington, the National Capital*, 1932.

Carroll, E. M., *Origins of the Whig Party*, 1925.

Calhoun, John C., *Works*, ed. by Richard K. Crallé, 1854.

Channing, Edward, *A History of the United States, 1700-1861*, 1905-25.

Clay, Henry, *The Works of Henry Clay*, ed. by Calvin Colton, 1904.

Clay, Thomas Hart, *Henry Clay*, 1910.

Dangerfield, George, *The Era of Good Feelings*, 1952.

Dallas, Susan (ed.), *Diary of George Mifflin Dallas*, 1892.

Eaton, Peggy, *Autobiography*, ed. by C. F. Deems, 1932.

Federal Writers' Project, American Guide Series, *Washington, City and Capital*, 1937.

Fowler, Harlan D., *Camels to California*, 1950.

Frémont, Jessie Benton, *Souvenirs of My Time*, 1887.

Gallatin, James, *The Diary of James Gallatin*, ed. by Count Gallatin, 1924.

Gilman, Daniel C., *James Monroe*, 1895.

Gouverneur, Marian, *As I Remember, Recollections of American Society during the Nineteenth Century*, 1911.

Graham, G. S., *Sea Power and British North America 1783-1820*, 1941.

Hamilton, Holman, *Zachary Taylor*, 1951.

Hamlin, Teunis S., *Historic Houses of Washington*, 1893.

Heap, Gwinn Harris, *Central Route to the Pacific from the Valley of the Mississippi to California: Journal of the Expedition of E. F. Beale, Superintendent of Indian Affairs in California, and Gwinn Harris Heap, from Missouri to California, in 1853*, 1854.

Higginson, T. W., *Travellers and Outlaws*, 1889.

Hunt, Charles H., *Life of Livingston*, 1864.

Hyde de Neuville, *Mémoires et Souvenirs du Baron Hyde de Neuville*, 1892; Eng. trans. by Francis Jackson, London, 1913.

Jackson, Andrew, *Correspondence, ed. by J. S. Bassett*, 1926-33.

James, Marquis, *Andrew Jackson, Portrait of a President*, 1937.

Johnson, Willis F., *America's Foreign Relations*, 1921.

Latrobe, Benjamin Henry, *Journal*, 1905.

——, *Impressions Respecting New Orleans*, ed. by Samuel Wilson Jr., 1951.

Latané, John H. and D. W. Wainhouse, *A History of American Foreign Policy*, 1934.

Lesley, Lewis Burt, *Uncle Sam's Camels*, 1929.

Lewis, C. L., *The Romantic Decatur*, 1937.

Lockwood, Mary Smith, *Yesterdays in Washington*, n. d.

Lynch, Dennis T., *An Epoch and a Man; Martin Van Buren and His Times*, 1929.

Mackenzie, A. S., *Life of Stephen Decatur*, 1846.

Mahan, A. T., *Sea Power in Its Relations to the War of 1812*, 1905.

McMaster, John Bach, *The History of the People of the United States From the Revolution to the Civil War*, 1883-1913.

Martineau, Harriet, *Retrospect of Western Travel*, 1838.

Mayo, Bernard, *Henry Clay: Spokesman of the New West*, 1937.

Meade, Robert D., *Judah P. Benjamin, Confederate Statesman*, 1943.

Meigs, W. M., *The Life of Thomas Hart Benton*, 1904.

——, *The Life of John Caldwell Calhoun*, 1917.

Meyer, Balthasar H., *History of Transportation in the United States before 1860*, 1917.

Morison, Samuel Eliot and H. S. Commager, *The Growth of the American Republic*, 1942.

Osterweis, Rollin, *Judah P. Benjamin*, 1933.

Paullin, C. O., "Duelling in the Old Navy," in *United States Naval Institute Proceedings*, vol. xxxv, 1184.

Perkins, Dexter, *The Monroe Doctrine, 1823-1826*, 1927.

Porter, David D., *Memoir of Commodore David Porter*, 1875.

Quincy, Josiah P., *Figures of the Past*, 1883.

Schlesinger, Arthur M., Jr., *The Age of Jackson*, 1945.

Singleton, Esther, *The Story of the White House*, 1907.

Smith, Margaret Bayard (Mrs. Samuel Harrison Smith), *The First Forty Years of Washington Society*, ed. by Gaillard Hunt, 1906.

Sumner, William G., *Andrew Jackson*, 1882.

Tatum, Edward L., *The United States and Europe, 1815-1823*, 1936.

Tayloe, Benjamin Ogle, *In Memoriam*, 1872.

Taylor, Bayard, *Adventures and Life in San Francisco*, 1852.

Thomas, Benjamin Platt, *Russo-American Relations 1815-1867*, 1930.

United States Navy, *Naval Documents Related to the United States Wars with the Barbary Powers*, 1939-42.

Van Deusen, G. G., *The Life of Henry Clay*, 1937.

Waldo, Samuel Putnam, *The Life and Character of Stephen Decatur*, 1821.

Watson, P. B., *The Tragic Career of Commodore James Barron*, 1942.

Westcott, Allan (ed), *American Sea Power Since 1775*, 1947.

Whitton, Mary O., *First First Ladies 1789-1865*, 1948.

Willson, Beckles, *Friendly Relations*, 1934.

156

10 feet high, clear of the plinth which receives the upper & lower lining of the Cap.

10 in
8 in

2.6

2.6